BEFRIEND GOD: LIFE WITH JESUS

Howard Storm

Copyright © 2017 Howard Storm
All rights reserved.

The painting on the cover is by Howard Storm.

Scripture quotations are from New Revised Standard Version Bible (NRSV), copyright © 1989 National Council of the Churches of Christ in the United States of America. Used by permission. All rights reserved worldwide.

TABLE OF CONTENTS

Introduction		v
Chapter 1	The Cosmic Christ	1
Chapter 2	The Jesus of Faith	9
Chapter 3	Jesus and the Church	17
Chapter 4	The Person of Jesus	32
Chapter 5	The Passion	50
Chapter 6	His Love	64
Chapter 7	His Forgiveness	71
Chapter 8	Women and Jesus	77
Chapter 9	His Commandments	89
Chapter 10	His Promise	100
Chapter 11	Prayer	107
Chapter 12	Miracles	118
Chapter 13	Called	127
Chapter 14	Discipleship	134
Chapter 15	Judgment	143
Chapter 16	Eternal Life	151
Chapter 17	Salvation	158
Chapter 18	The Kingdom of God	167
Chapter 19	The Enemy	178
Chapter 20	Heaven and Hell	187

INTRODUCTION

Jesus is the physical incarnation of the creative activity of God. The Christ always existed from the beginning of creation. He became human for a brief time, two thousand years ago, in the evolving human consciousness to radically change the spiritual development of humankind. Humanity desperately needed a Savior. With the rapidly growing empires in the East and the West, humanity was becoming increasingly brutal and hedonistic. The appearance of Jesus was at the precise right time and at the precise right place at the crossroads of three continents. The Cosmic Christ has continued to interact with humans through the Spirit of Christ, who has been sent by God to guide and empower our spiritual progress. After Jesus' ascension into heaven, he specifically told his disciples to receive the Holy Spirit who would further his work in the world. The Holy Spirit has been working to continue the spiritual work of Jesus ever since, through the Christian church, and through individuals.

The Spirit of Christ has been actively involved with humans from the beginning of creation. The reception of the Spirit of God has been erratic in human understanding. Everything good, everything loving, and everything beautiful has been inspired by this Spirit of Christ. There are numerous sources of inspiration but there is only one Holy Spirit. What we credit as human achievement in the arts, science, medicine, philosophy, etc. is the inspiration of the Holy Spirit. The Spirit of Christ continues today to guide us into being the people that God created us to be.

The purpose in writing this book is for all people to know Jesus Christ, and receive his love so that they may join all the Saints in heaven. It is God's fervent desire that not one soul be lost. Jesus Christ is the Savior of the world and there is no other. In God's great love for humankind, we have been given the freedom to choose to receive this love and truth or not. When we ask to receive the Spirit of Christ in our hearts to be our Savior, we know whether we have been sincere or not. And if we have asked sincerely, we know that we have received the Spirit of Christ and our lives will be changed. If we belong to him, we will always belong to him and he will never lose us. Jesus Christ is the way, the truth, and the life. He promises us eternal life when we put our faith in him. May you know Him as your personal Savior and Lord of your life.

Saint Paul has eloquently expressed what knowing Jesus Christ has meant to me and to all people who truly know him in the following words: "Yet whatever gains I had, these I have come to regard as loss because of Christ. More than that, I regard everything as loss because of the surpassing value of knowing Christ Jesus my Lord. For his sake I have suffered the loss of all things, and I regard them as rubbish, in order that I may gain Christ and be found in him, not having a righteousness of my own that comes from the law, but one that comes through faith in Christ, the righteousness from God based on faith. I want to know Christ and the power of his resurrection and the sharing of his sufferings by becoming like him in his death, if somehow I may attain the resurrection from the dead," Philippians 3:7-12 (NRSV).

The Christian is a person who follows Jesus Christ. Every Christian is in the process of knowing him better, so there are baby Christians, infant Christians, childlike Christians, teenage Christians, mature Christians, and wise Christians. This is the process of sanctification that is the reason for our existence. Going to church does not make one Christian. Knowing about Jesus does not make one Christian. Thinking that you are a good person does not make you a Christian. The only way that you can be a Christian is to have the Spirit of Christ in your heart. The Spirit of Christ will only come into your heart when he is invited and we are obedient to the Spirit. The chief characteristic of the Spirit of Christ is the revelation of truth that Jesus is the chosen one of God. You will know him by his love. He knows you better than you know yourself.

This book is written so that we will know God and His will more clearly as it has been revealed in the person of Jesus. This is a simple guide to understanding topics that would require volumes to be definitive. My hope is to speak to the widest range of people seeking the truth about God and Jesus. There are many greater than myself who have written libraries of scholarly works on these subjects. My purpose is to spread the Good News to anyone interested. It is my belief that my understanding is consistent with the majority of Christian doctrine for the past centuries. It is my intention to lead people into a church where their spiritual growth will be shepherded by a congregation of believers and they will excel in love, hope, and faith.

What God requires of us is not difficult to understand. The People of Israel knew this for more than a thousand years before Jesus. Jesus said, the first commandment is, "Hear, O Israel: the Lord our God, the Lord is one; you shall love the Lord your God with all your heart, and with all your soul, and with all your mind, and with all your strength," Mark 12:29-30 (NRSV).

How is this possible? With God's help, this is possible. Without the help of God, it is impossible. The self-revelation of God has been known, obscured, perverted, and misused by many peoples over the centuries. To make perfect the revelation of God, God came to us in the incarnation of Jesus. Jesus and God are one and the same. See John 14:6 (NRSV), when Jesus said, "I am the way, and the truth, and the life. No one comes to the Father except through me." In John 14:6, he was stating the fact of his complete unity with God. This statement tells us the path to God is following what Jesus taught. This is an absolute truth and will never be changed.

When I was thirty-eight years old, this fact completely changed my life. Ever since that time, it has been the singular focus of my life of how to live a life pleasing to God. This journey has been an adventure I could never have imagined. There have been miracles, abysmal failures, times of joy, and times of sorrow. During these decades, God has been growing me and disciplining me like a loving parent. So I have to thank God for all of it, both the good and the bad.

Perhaps the most difficult thing in the world to change is the human soul. That is precisely what God wants to transform and what has been happening to me. A simple way to express this is opening the heart of compassion. Jesus added a second great commandment to the first, "You shall love your neighbor as yourself," Mark 12:31 (NRSV). Loving God includes loving God's creatures, and that means every person on this planet. Impossible? Without the love of God it cannot happen, and with the universal love of God an amazing new reality will be realized. The Kingdom of Heaven will be on earth. God demands we demonstrate our love of God with our love for God's people. This can be quite challenging at times and very gratifying at other times. Obedience requires us to love our sisters and brothers all the time. How our love is expressed is the question we face every minute of every day and there is never a uniform answer. Living in the moment of listening to the Spirit of Christ is the way to find the inspiration of how we need to interact with our fellow creatures. This is why we are so fortunate to have Jesus as our model and guide. Jesus interacted in every type of situation, and we can be instructed by his example. Everything we encounter he also encountered. Following Jesus is the path of having a right relationship with God. We are not alone in this world. May we walk together on this journey and discover the truth of God.

You believe in something. Everyone believes in something. Total apathy becomes inertia which inevitably leads to death. The difference that defines people is what they believe, which motivates their life. The foundational object of a person's belief is their god. Although one can claim they are an atheist, there is no such viable belief system because everyone believes in and worships something. Materialism is a form of religion. The critical question of every life is, what do you believe? What do you trust, adore, worship, and seek? This is your god/God.

Jesus Christ, who is the most recognized individual on earth, asks us to surrender all of our beliefs and believe in him above all other objects of our desire. He is the most radical belief since he asks for everything and promises no worldly reward in return. Jesus is the most rewarding experience of a life for those who do know him. Those who do not know him are oblivious to the sublime heights of love shared between his intimate acquaintances and his self. This book is written to describe what cannot be stated with words, but can only be experienced. The ineffable nature of his love is the most powerful force in the universe. So one can only point towards it and suggest its attributes and effect on one's life. Since every person craves to find the meaning and purpose in their existence, it is better to point in the right direction than to ignore the random striving of our sisters and brothers. The way is Jesus. The truth is Jesus. Life is Jesus. Jesus and God are One.

ACKNOWLEDGEMENTS

This book was many years in the making. It was made possible by the love and support of two women. My wife Marcia has been my best companion and has always given me her love and faithfulness. She has been an amazing gift from God and I am grateful more than she may know. Anne Steinemann has been more than an editor and constant driver of completing this book and she has contributed in critical ways to keep to the task. Would I ever have finished if it were not for the gentle persuasion of Anne. We only know each other through Skype but we are truly brother and sister in Christ Jesus. God sends angels to help us and I have been blessed with many but two are flesh and blood that I have been privileged to know and love.

ABOUT THE AUTHOR

Howard Storm was born October 26, 1946, in Newton, Massachusetts. He was raised in the suburbs of Boston and summers on Cape Cod. He received his BFA from The San Francisco Art Institute, MA and MFA from the University of California, Berkeley, and MDiv from United Theological Seminary. He was a Professor of Art at Northern Kentucky University for twenty years and served as Pastor in the United Church of Christ for thirty years. He is the author of "My Descent Into Death," "It's All Love," and "Lessons Learned." He is married to Marcia Storm and they live in Kentucky with their sweet Boykin Spaniels. The "Near Death Experience" on June 1, 1985, completely changed the course of his life and he has been trying to live a life pleasing to God ever since.

CHAPTER 1

THE COSMIC CHRIST

Jesus, son of Joseph and Mary of Nazareth, was a flesh and blood man who lived in Roman occupied Israel during the tyranny of the Roman Empire. His origins were as humble as could be. His upbringing in Nazareth was subsistence existence. He never owned anything except the clothes he wore, never carried money, and was a hunted man during his three years of ministry. He lived some thirty years and was crucified as a despised criminal. From worldly appearances, this was a perfectly unremarkable existence. Curiously, this man was the most important world-changing individual to ever have existed. How is this possible?

From the perspective of faith in Jesus Christ, this is simply more of the evidence that he was truly the Chosen One of God, the Messiah, and the Christ. From a perspective of faithlessness, it is all a matter of lucky coincidences and delusions. The cynical view has nothing of value to contribute to our understanding of Jesus as the Cosmic Christ, so we must rely upon the testimony of faith. How was Jesus the man, also the Cosmic Christ?

The first and comprehensive salvo of understanding of the Cosmic Christ is the opening verses of the Gospel of John 1:1-3 (NRSV): "In the beginning was the Word, and the Word was with

God, and the Word was God. He was in the beginning with God. All things came into being through him, and without him not one thing came into being." We have come to understand the "Word" of God is the same as Jesus. So we have two Jesus who are not different but the same. One is the Jesus who was born, lived, died, and was resurrected. The other Jesus is the "Word" of God. The Word of God means the thought and action of God. In the original Greek text, the word is "logos," which translates as thought action. So Jesus was both the man of flesh who lived with us, and Jesus is the personal name for the thought and activity of God. We identify Christ as the procreative work of God in the universe.

Looking into the scriptural testimony about God, we see the Cosmic Christ in the beginning. In Genesis 1:1-2 (NRSV), "In the beginning when God created the heavens and the earth, the earth was a formless void and darkness covered the face of the deep, while a wind from God swept over the face of the waters." The Cosmic Christ is this creative action of God creating and hovering. And the presence of Christ is always the creative thought action of the creation. "All things came into being through him," John 1:3 (NRSV). Theoretical physicists understand this act of creation of the physical universe as the "big bang." The big bang was God sending forth the Word. Saint John understood that this event of the creation was an expression of love and light that would later be revealed in the person of Jesus. Before the singularity of the "big bang," all the laws of physics existed, which is common scientific knowledge. The Christ was the laws of physics before the universe was created.

It is intellectually challenging to move from the Cosmic Christ to the incarnate Christ. Wonderfully they converge in Jesus and then diverge again into the Jesus Christ of the faith. The tradition calls this one of the great mysteries of the faith. A mystery is something that cannot be adequately expressed in language, but can be appreciated at a deeper level of understanding. For example, a mystery like love is ineffable, but absolutely essential to life and profoundly experienced. To perfectly comprehend the incarnation of the divine in the human is to perfectly comprehend God, and that is not within the capacity of human intelligence. God's creative expression of self is in the creation in part, but not in total. Is there any reason to believe that God could not express God's nature and will in a human? If God can make the universe, God can express God's self in Jesus of Nazareth.

The enormous discovery of the disciples of Jesus was that Jesus the man was the revelation of God in human form. There was no existing language to adequately express this, so the language that approximated the unique relationship of Jesus to God was used. Jesus was called the Son of God. He was called the Messiah in Hebrew, or the Christ in Greek. This carried nuances of different meanings but clearly stated that he was the "Chosen One" of God to show the way. Unfortunately, differing expectations of the role of a Messiah caused conflict and confusion about who Jesus was and what he was expected to do. The term Son of God in English implies some biological relationship, which is absurd because God is not a biological being. The term derives from the Hebrew "ben" meaning to be from. It can mean son, made by, from, or product of. Jesus was all of these and more, but none could capture the true nature of the relationship of Jesus to God. We most often rely upon the metaphor of father to son because it was the way Jesus described himself. What he was stating was the intimacy of his self with that of God. In fact, their intimacy was closer than a father to a son. Jesus even used the most informal and intimate form to address God, calling God "Abba," which would be daddy or papa in English. There is no human equivalent for the unity of will and nature that existed between Jesus and God except to say that they were one being in two different forms or persons.

In the Gospel of John, we have other theological attempts to express the nature of Jesus. In John 1:4-5 (NRSV), "In him was life, and the life was the light of all people. The light shines in the darkness, and the darkness did not overcome it." The images of God's expression of self in words like life and light are deeply grounded in the tradition of the Hebrew Scriptures. Jesus also frequently used these words to identify himself. Jesus uses the word life as his identification with God in John 5:26, 6:35, 8:12, and 14:6. Jesus refers to himself as the light in John 8:12, 9:5, 12:35, and 12:36. Jesus knew he was the light of God. He was the life God gives. He could not have said it more clearly that he was the revelation of God. Jesus said in John 8:12 (NRSV), "I am the light of the world. Whoever follows me will never walk in darkness but will have the light of life." The light of God is perhaps the perfect expression of who Jesus is and his relationship to God. If God is the sun, then Jesus is the sunlight. The claims of Jesus are unique in the history of the world. There has never been a sane and credible teacher, prophet, or guru who has made such claims about himself.

It was known by Jesus and his disciples that the enormity and importance of his revelation of God was going to meet with strong resistance. Because of the pride and perversity of human nature, most humans were not willing to accept a Savior of such humility and simplicity. To most, the love of God demonstrated in the life and teachings of Jesus were not grandiose enough to feed self-centered needs. Jesus did not feed the egos of humans; rather, he declared war upon the excesses of the human ego. John 1:9-12 states, "The true light that gives light to every man was coming into the world. He was in the world, and though the world was made through him, the world did not recognize him. He came to that which was his own, but his own did not receive him. Yet to all who received him, to those who believed in his name, he gave the right to become children of God." Humans were long used to men who claimed divinity, but rarely did the narcissus deceive anyone. Jesus sought nothing from people except love, and accepted nothing except faith. There was no precedent for the divine incarnation that was Jesus, and his self-sacrificing love.

1 John 4:8 (NRSV) states, "Whoever does not love does not know God, for God is love." Jesus as the complete revelation of God was love. One can define him very simply: Jesus is love. Regrettably, there were and are few people who are primarily motivated by love and are capable of the love God has given us.

This unconditional love called "agape" is different than sentimental love, brotherly love, sexual love, or other worldly forms of love. Saint Paul writes to the Philippians 2:1-5 (NRSV), "If then there is any encouragement in Christ, any consolation from love, any sharing in the Spirit, any compassion and sympathy, make my joy complete: be of the same mind, having the same love, being in full accord and of one mind. Do nothing from selfish ambition or conceit, but in humility regard others as better than yourselves. Let each of you look not to your own interests, but to the interests of others. Let the same mind be in you that was in Christ Jesus." The agape of God and Jesus is strikingly different than the types of love known in the Roman Empire. The Roman Empire was based on domination and exploitation of others. Jesus taught a love that was self-sacrificing, putting the needs of others ahead of ones' own needs. The world tried to murder the love Jesus taught, but could not. Agape cannot be killed because love is eternal, and love is from God. This is why they can kill the body but not the soul.

The Bread of Life is another way that Jesus described himself. In John 6:35 (NRSV), "Jesus said to them, 'I am the bread of life. Whoever comes to me will never be hungry, and whoever believes in me will never be thirsty.'" Bread represents sustenance for life. We are taught to pray for our daily bread. This is praying for the sustenance of life. Jesus also instituted a sacrament of Holy Communion with us, using bread as the medium for partaking of his nature, and wine becomes his life. Bread and wine become the Spirit of God invited into our life. The simplicity of the communion elements becomes the spiritual reality of God with us and in us.

The Good Shepherd is another traditional image for God that Jesus uses to describe his self. In John 10:11 (NRSV), Jesus proclaims, "I am the good shepherd. The good shepherd lays down his life for the sheep." This image of God is widely known from sources in the Hebrew Scriptures such as Psalm 23, "The Lord is my shepherd." Jesus used the metaphor of the shepherd and the sheep to describe his compassion for people several times. A few of the references are Matthew 9:36 and 25:32, Mark 6:34, and John 10:14. The image of Jesus as the good shepherd is one of the earliest painted images of Jesus we have from ancient Rome. Jesus cares for us, provides for us, and protects us from evil. He is present in our lives and wants an intimate relationship with us.

When Jesus was tortured, crucified, died, and buried, it appeared that his mission was a complete failure. His disciples were dispersed and in hiding. He had left behind no written record of his teachings. There was no organization or apparent structure to carry on his work. The Jesus movement appeared dead. To the amazement of everyone, upon his resurrection, he began a movement that swept through the hostile Roman Empire in a few centuries. Although the earthly life of Jesus was a mere thirty years, his ministry was three years, his followers numbered a few hundred, and as his life ended with his execution as a criminal, the ministry was just beginning. The darkness did not overcome the light. The power of sin and death did not defeat life. In fact, the light was shining more brightly in the world than it had ever done before. The power of sin and death had been destroyed by the forgiveness won by Christ Jesus' atonement for our sin. And finally death was swallowed up in life. He showed his disciples his power over death by his resurrection, and promised his disciples eternal life in heaven. The light of life had shown fully for the first time in the world in Christ Jesus' resurrection. Human existence now had a completely new and different meaning. A person could be freed from their slavery to sin. A person could rely upon the promise and perfection of God's Chosen One to receive eternal life. This new understanding of life was available to anyone who chose the way of Jesus, which is the way of faith, hope, and love. Jesus' death and resurrection was the triumph of the light of God.

Can a human grasp the connection between the Christ as the creative activity of God, the incarnation of the word of God in the fully human Jesus of Nazareth, and the living presence of the Spirit of Christ in our hearts and minds? This Trinitarian understanding of the Holy One is the basis for comprehension of this mystery. The Spirit of Christ leads us to the person of Jesus, and Jesus leads us into the very heart of God. This is God's plan. It is not a cleverly devised human construct. God has created this revelation so that we may do God's will on earth as it is in heaven, and so we may become part of the heavenly realm. The more you learn and think about God's plan for the salvation of the world, the more it makes sense. It is entirely rational and appeals to the intellect as well as the heart. The more one participates in God's plan, the more love, hope, and faith we experience on a daily basis. As science reveals more of the details and secrets of the universe, we are given increasing insight into the Designer of all that is. Everything reveals the glory of the Holy One.

What we believe is always a choice that we make. Our perception of reality, the culture that shaped us, and the desires that drive us are important factors in our lives, but we have the capacity to make choices every moment of our lives. The choice to deny God and presume that we are our own masters is a bankrupt philosophy in our personal development as spiritual beings and is an obstacle to the development of a more loving and hospitable world. Our choices have consequences we can't imagine. Living in an abiding faith connects us to the Creator and the creation in ways that engage our entire being. The mysteries are no longer threats, but we embrace them in love because the mysteries have embraced us in love. The cosmic Christ appears to us as a sweet man who has nothing but our best interests in his mind. He gives us as much love as we can handle and shares his joy and peace with us. When we know him we want to share the benefits of knowing him with everyone. See the symbols, see the rituals, hear the words, taste the sweetness of the music, enjoy the fellowship, and share this with the broken men and women. It is wonderful beyond words. Do you want to know God? Come and see Jesus.

CHAPTER 2
THE JESUS OF FAITH

The Jesus of faith has been given to us by the testimonies in the scriptures, the doctrines and traditions of the church, and personal experiences of millions of people who have known Jesus. Since he is the most important human who has ever lived, more has been written about him, and more has been said about him, than any other human being. Jesus has been terribly misunderstood and abused through no fault of his own. Regardless of human frailty, what he came into the world to do, he accomplished. Ever since, he has guided humans to become children of God. He has sent his Spirit to dwell in us so that we may be like him, as sons and daughters of God. Jesus is a living being, who for two thousand years, billions have learned to trust, believe, and put their faith in completely.

The revelation of God has been unfolding throughout human history, and culminated in the life of Jesus Christ. In God's own plan and time, the very nature of God was revealed in Jesus. In the study of world religions, it is remarkable how confused and contradictory has been the understanding of the nature of God. In many religions, God has been portrayed as a monster who can only be appeased with blood. Every evil has been ascribed to God, and used to justify the most horrible human actions. God has ended the mystery and the debate by coming to us in human form, teaching us the truth, and showing us the way. Jesus is the prototype for how humans should treat each other and how we are to relate to God. Jesus, for the first time in history, brought full divinity into humanity. He was the first, and he was unique. There has never been another like him. No other human being has done what he did. And this was done so that we could become like him and live with him in heaven. Jesus is the perfect revelation of God. In John 14:9-11 (NRSV), "Jesus said to him, 'Have I been with you all this time, Philip, and you still do not know me? Whoever has seen me has seen the Father. How can you say, "Show us the Father"? Do you not believe that I am in the Father and the Father is in me? The words that I say to you I do not speak on my own; but the Father who dwells in me does his works. Believe me that I am in the Father and the Father is in me; but if you do not, then believe me because of the works themselves.'" He wants us to have the love of God as he gave us that love. He wants us to have the same intimacy with him as he had with God. God came to us so that we could come to God. This is what life is all about, and Jesus is the means that makes it possible.

The Spirit of God has been experienced at times by people throughout history. Jesus who was filled with a Holy Spirit sent his Holy Spirit to his disciples so that they would have the power to proclaim the truth throughout the whole world. Jesus promised the Spirit of God to his disciples and the church has been empowered by that Spirit ever since. The very existence of the church is dependent upon the work of the Holy Spirit drawing people to Jesus and into the community of the church. It is the gift of faith that the Holy Spirit gives that brings people into relationship with Jesus Christ and into the community of the church. Faith and truth in Jesus Christ is the primary work of the Holy Spirit. John 16:7-15 (NRSV), "Nevertheless I tell you the truth: it is to your advantage that I go away, for if I do not go away, the Advocate will not come to you; but if I go, I will send him to you. And when he comes, he will prove the world wrong about sin and righteousness and judgment: about sin, because they do not believe in me; about righteousness, because I am going to the Father and you will see me no longer; about judgment, because the ruler of this world has been condemned. I still have many things to say to you, but you cannot bear them now. When the Spirit of truth comes, he will guide you into all the truth; for he will not speak on his own, but will speak whatever he hears, and he will declare to you the things that are to come. He will glorify me, because he will take what is mine and declare it to you. All that the Father has is mine. For this reason I said that he will take what is mine and declare it to you."

Some of the facts about the historical Jesus are elusive because the only information we have about his life was written by four believers who wrote to propagate the faith in Jesus Christ. Although there is biographical material in the Gospels, the intention of the Gospel writers was not to be biographers or historians. The authors of the Gospels wrote for the sole purpose of bringing people into faith and into relationship with Jesus Christ as Savior. The Gospels were written directly from first-hand accounts of his disciples. No one can prove or disprove the accuracy of the Gospels. Any critique of them as reliable is a measure of the faith or disbelief of the critic. If we believe Jesus Christ is the Son of God, and we believe that he directly sent his Spirit to guide his disciples, then we believe that the Gospels are the truth that he inspired them to write for our salvation. If we believe Jesus Christ is who he says he is, we believe that he is more than capable of doing this for us. The Gospels are about truth. The truth that they teach is revealing the truth about God. The historical facts about the life of Jesus are relatively insignificant in comparison to the theological truth about Jesus. The Jesus of faith is far more important than the Jesus of history.

There exists today a large amount of archaeological evidence to support the credibility of the Gospel writers. But there will never be enough evidence to convince an unbeliever. Faith is not something that can be proven, nor can it be given. Faith comes from God. It has the same elusive and incomprehensible quality as love. This is no coincidence, since faith and love are two sides of the same coin. When a skeptic examines the Gospels, he finds little of value and much confusion. When a person of faith examines the Gospels, he finds the living Word of God. The more one studies the Gospels in faith, the more real and alive Jesus becomes. The historical Jesus becomes the living Jesus. He speaks to us, he teaches us, he heals us, he saves us, and he loves us through the Gospels.

Faith is a conscious decision to adopt a system of premises that may have a supporting factual basis. Everyone has a faith system that allows them to function. We live by faith the sun will rise after the night. We live by faith that people will obey the laws and we will be safe. We live by faith that our family loves us and protects us. We live by faith that the cash register at the store does not rob us. One could cite thousands of examples of faith statements that are taken as true for most people most of the time. When a belief we hold to be true is proven to be untrue, it is traumatic. This trauma can be the lifelong inability to trust many things. The root cause of denial of God can be traced back to a trauma or multiple traumas in early development. How can a person have a trusting believing relationship with God when they have been betrayed by a parent? Trust, faith, and belief are essentially the same and can be devastated by trauma.

The Gospels contain the truth about Jesus Christ. There is precisely the right amount of information for us to know him. There is neither too little nor too much information. The Holy Spirit inspired the Gospel writers with the testimony of the disciples that needed to be told. Jesus did much more in his life in this world that we do not need to know at this time. In John 21:25 (NRSV), "But there are also many other things that Jesus did; if every one of them were written down, I suppose that the world itself could not contain the books that would be written." The complete story of the life of Jesus in this world would be overwhelming. The story of Jesus working in the lives of the people who have lived since his time would fill billions of books. The relevant question for us is, how does our story intersect with his story? How do we identify with various characters in the Gospel stories? How is our faith shaped by the words and deeds of Jesus?

The living presence of Jesus is the reason why Christianity exists today. It was the living presence of Christ that sent the first apostles out into the world and gave them the words to speak which changed lives. It was the living Spirit who worked through them that brought more people to Jesus and created the church. The Spirit of Christ gave them the courage to persevere under every persecution the Roman Empire could devise, and they prevailed. They knew Jesus as a real living presence in their lives. In Matthew 18:20 (NRSV), "For where two or three are gathered in my name, I am there among them." The disciples of Jesus are never apart from the master. Even if we are unfaithful, he is always faithful. When we give ourselves to him, he will never abandon us. In Matthew 28:20 (NRSV), "And remember, I am with you always, to the end of the age." Wherever we go in the name of Jesus, we are never alone.

The moment you meet Jesus is the day that everything in your life begins to change. Fear becomes hope, hate becomes love, doubt becomes belief, worry becomes confidence, and despair becomes joy. Jesus meets us where we are, but he does not leave us where we are, because he loves us so much he will not be indifferent to our inadequacy. He helps us mature from our worldly nature into the spiritual nature. This process takes more than a lifetime, but with Jesus we have all the time in the universe to realize our fullest potential. In the Gospels, we see that even his closest disciples had a lot of growing up to do. When Peter met the resurrected Christ, he was being prepared for a lifetime of ministry.

John 21:15-17 (NRSV): "When they had finished breakfast, Jesus said to Simon Peter, 'Simon son of John, do you love me more than these?' He said to him, 'Yes, Lord; you know that I love you.' Jesus said to him, 'Feed my lambs.' A second time he said to him, 'Simon son of John, do you love me?' He said to him, 'Yes, Lord; you know that I love you.' Jesus said to him, 'Tend my sheep.' He said to him the third time, 'Simon son of John, do you love me?' Peter felt hurt because he said to him the third time, 'Do you love me?' And he said to him, 'Lord, you know everything; you know that I love you.' Jesus said to him, 'Feed my sheep.'" Like Peter, we will be asked, "Do you love me? Feed my sheep."

Following Jesus involves both a change of heart and a change of life. We are asked to love God, and to love our neighbors as ourselves. The way of love is the most difficult, most dangerous, and most wonderful way of life there is. That is what every follower of Jesus knows. Faith in Jesus is to live a life that pleases God, which means our entire thoughts, words, and deeds. To claim a belief in Jesus, and living apart from his commandments to go and serve in his name, is hypocrisy. The commandment to love is a call to action and not a description of sentiment. In Matthew 28:19-20 (NRSV), "Go therefore and make disciples of all nations, baptizing them in the name of the Father and of the Son and of the Holy Spirit, and teaching them to obey everything I have commanded you." To ignore this is to receive the same fate as the people in Matthew 25:45-46 (NRSV). If you are not familiar with these verses, you need to be.

Faith is a gift from God and can be increased by asking God for more faith. In Matthew 7:11 (NRSV), "How much more will your Father in heaven give good gifts to those who ask him!" Faith is one of the good gifts Jesus wants us to ask for repeatedly. To assume you have sufficient faith in Jesus is proof that your faith is insufficient. The more we know him, love him, and trust him, the more we desire. Our heart craves closeness to him always. This is the nature of being in love with someone. Jesus is a living being and desires a passionate love in response to his love. Thankfully, we have the opportunity to worship where we can unashamedly express our faith in music, teaching, and prayer. The faith experience during worship is invigorating. I compare it to having our battery charged. The conflicts and discouragements we are confronted with daily deplete the joy and peace of our faith and necessitate renewal frequently. Worship fills us with an overflowing of the cup of the Spirit of Christ. It is difficult to comprehend why some Christians claim they don't need worship in the Body of Christ. There is a serious difference between corporate worship and individual worship. Both are invaluable but the differences are significant. Corporate worship is indispensable in the spiritual journey of faith.

Our brains have an emotional half and a rational half. They are both necessary and need to be balanced. Faith emotionally experienced is just as important as intellectual faith. The example of Jesus is addressed to both reason and emotion. To believe in him is to pursue knowledge and understanding of him and to love and adore him. It is unhealthy to be one-sided in either direction. Reason and emotions are tools for the development of our souls, and they are not who we are. To cast our identity into defining ourselves as feeling or thoughts is a disservice and delusional to our being. Jesus wants all of us and he wants us healthy and not a false self-image.

It is good to wrestle with doubts. As long as we are searching for truth, the Gospels cannot only survive the deepest scrutiny, but they will also give us wisdom and knowledge that we never expected. Take all your doubts to the Holy Spirit and ask for understanding and you will find the answers. Sometimes it happens fast and other times it takes years. The fact is when you search you will find, and when you ask the answer will be given. Without doubts, you are assuming things without using reason to understand why a notion is true or untrue. After we have subjected a concept to a critical think, we believe it more deeply and can explain why we believe it to another. We are called to make disciples and to teach; therefore, we must know why we believe our faith and explain it to an unbeliever. Doubt builds a stronger faith so it is nothing to be feared because it produces good fruits.

It is good to feel estranged from God. Would it be best for us to feel in the presence of God every minute of our life? That is what we will enjoy in heaven. While in this world, we feel periods of estrangement and periods of God's presence. The absence motivates us for more intimacy with God. It is part of our human nature to become complacent when there is no struggle. We are in this world to develop as spiritual beings and complacency is contrary to growth. God never gives us more than we can bear, but God gives us challenges to overcome. This school of life is experiential learning and we are tested frequently. Let the times of spiritual dryness be times of growth and maturing. Romans 8:28 (NRSV) informs us, "We know that all things work together for good for those who love God, who are called according to his purpose." We stand firm in our faith in all seasons.

The faith in Jesus is what we have been given by God for the salvation of the world. The gift is only meaningful when we use it to glorify God in service to the world. Our response to the Jesus of faith, this most precious of all gifts, is to share the anointing that overflows from our heart.

CHAPTER 3

JESUS AND THE CHURCH

If there were no church, there would be no Christianity, there would be no Bible, and there would be no Christians. The church established by Jesus Christ called diverse groups of people together to form communities and in time these became institutions. The Jewish community gathered sacred scriptures together and formed the Hebrew Testaments, which were preserved and revered by the early Christians, and they began to collect texts that were eventually preserved and revered as the New Testament. Without the church, most or possibly all these scriptures would have been lost over time as has been the fate of most of the writings of ancient times. Without the church and the Bible, who would know anything about Christianity? The influence of the church is incalculable. I love the church in all its dimensions and have devoted my life to maintaining, building, and spreading the church in the world. This is what Jesus commanded us to do.

Humans in the Church
The church has been at different times the best friend and the adversary of Jesus Christ. At other times, it has been both faithful and foe simultaneously. Jesus initiated the church, the Holy Spirit

inspired it, and humans have built it. The church has at times represented the best of Christianity and the worst. Every human who walks in the door of the church brings with them all that is good and all that is evil inside of them. There is no security guard checking for spiritual terrorists at the door. Since we are responsible for the church, as it is, we have to bear the full responsibility for its triumphs and failures. Every church that claims Jesus Christ as its head proclaims its unique fidelity to the truth of Jesus Christ. Yet they are all flawed, far from perfection, and still the church is the best institution human can devise. What institution is not flawed by people? Is there a flawless government, educational system, business, hospital, or any other institution? If we could only have perfect people, we would have a perfect church. Each person, on every day, has the opportunity to recreate the church in the image of Jesus Christ.

Both the enemies and the friends of Jesus have not been negligent in pointing out the shortcomings and sins of the church. The opponents of the church use its failures as a reason to distrust it and discredit its founder. The friends of the church criticize it to seek its conformity to a more faithful understanding of who Jesus is and what he demands of his followers. The reformers have at times been just as misguided as the conservatives. They strain to uphold their traditions to the exclusion of others that have lost significance in the ever-changing culture. Honoring tradition and responding to the prevailing culture is a constant struggle in the church. The drama of the history of the church is both glorious and ignoble. This institution that spans two thousand years is as varied as the human history of this same period, not surprising since the same humans were involved in the making of both histories. The church is an integral part of culture and not separate from it.

The Called
Jesus calls us personally into his church. Faith is a two-way street. On one side, you have to be open and ready to receive the gift of

faith. On the other side, God has the exact right amount of faith to give at that moment. In Matthew 22:14 (NRSV), Jesus said, "For many are called, but few are chosen." Called into the church is a matter of timing, so the recipient of faith is ready when the grace of faith is available. Saint Paul writes in Romans 12:3 (NRSV), "For by the grace given to me I say to everyone among you not to think of yourself more highly than you ought to think, but to think with sober judgment, each according to the measure of faith that God has assigned." Some have received their faith growing up in a family and attending church. The faith they were given came with their mother's milk, and they cannot remember receiving it because it has always been there for them. Some receive their faith during a crisis and can name the minute and day they received their faith. Either way, we can take no credit for accepting faith in Jesus, other than we awoke from our stupor of ignorance and saw the light of the world for the first time. We are personally called by Jesus into the faith and into the church which is the Body of Christ.

The Body of Christ

The church was created to be the Body of Christ in this world. Saint Paul writes, "Now you are the body of Christ and individually members of it," 1 Corinthians 12:27 (NRSV). We are to incarnate the Spirit of Christ in our lives. But we have never been completely free from our worldly ways sufficiently to give the Spirit of Christ a full expression. Even the saints proclaim their failure. In Romans 7:18-24 (NRSV), Paul confesses, "For I know that nothing good dwells within me, that is, in my flesh. I can will what is right, but I cannot do it. For I do not do the good I want, but the evil I do not want is what I do. Now if I do what I do not want, it is no longer I that do it, but sin that dwells within me. So I find it to be a law that when I want to do what is good, evil lies close at hand. For I delight in the law of God in my inmost self, but I see in my members another law at war with the law of my mind, making me captive to the law of sin that dwells in my members. Wretched man that I am!

Who will rescue me from this body of death?" The problem with the church is not a theological problem; it is an anthropological problem.

Thankfully, the church is treated mercifully by its founder Jesus and is guided by the inspired faithful to be the Body of Christ. In defense of the church, it is typically less corrupt than other human institutions, and often represents the best of what humans are capable. Compared to other institutions of human endeavor, such as law, business, education, government, and medicine, the church has a remarkable history of functioning in a corrupt world in spite of every attempt to destroy it from within and without.

The church was instituted by Jesus to be his body in this world. The first function of the church is to observe the commandments of the law. Jesus was asked, "'Teacher, which commandment in the law is the greatest?' He said to him, '"You shall love the Lord your God with all your heart, and with all your soul, and with all your mind." This is the greatest and first commandment. And a second is like it: "You shall love your neighbor as yourself." On these two commandments hang all the law and the prophets.'" Matthew 22:36-40 (NRSV).

The church worships God. The corporate worship of God is more supernaturally important than most people know. It is not a question of whether God needs to be worshipped. The question is whether we need to worship God. Worship is our acknowledgement of God, and who God is. God is worthy of our praise. Life is out of balance without giving glory to the Creator and Source of Being. To give oneself in the corporate worship of God brings a person into "Higher Reality" even for a little while. Life devoid of worship of God is, at best, floundering through life. Church gives us the transcendent experience of corporate worship and has been doing that task for two thousand years for billions of people. This is one great way to love God with all you've got.

Church is training for life in heaven. If you don't like going to church, you are going to hate heaven. Church is a preview of what life in heaven is going to be like. There is no church building in heaven because heaven is church. The centerpiece of heaven is the worship of God, similar to how we sing the praise of God in church. It is no coincidence that music is central to praising God in virtually every church and temple in the world. Church is learning to live in harmony with our sisters and brothers as it is in heaven. Church is learning to be attentive to God and interacting with one another to become a symphony of praise in concert with the Supreme Being. This is one of the principal activities in heaven. Church teaches how to express the love of God.

The church has taught us to "Love your neighbor as yourself." The three critical words are love, neighbor, and yourself. As we define these three words, we fail or fulfill this commandment. We too often define love in terms that require little of us. To do "no harm" is not love. Love involves vulnerability, risk, effort, and sacrifice. The love of Christ is dangerous and we often avoid it. How have we loved as he loved us? The church tries to teach us how to love our neighbor as Jesus loved us.

Other than our family, who else has consistently taught us to love beside the church? Where else has love been proclaimed as the highest human virtue? It has only been the church extolling the primary importance of Christ's love. It has only been the church defining love as Christ's unselfish love. Where else will one hear 1 Corinthians Chapter 13 read over and over? The "love chapter" is the most important description of love in any language. "Love is patient; love is kind; love is not envious or boastful or arrogant or rude. It does not insist on its own way; it is not irritable or resentful; it does not rejoice in wrongdoing, but rejoices in the truth.It bears all things, believes all things, hopes all things, endures all things. Love never ends. But as for prophecies, they will come to an end; as for tongues, they will cease; as for knowledge, it will come to an end," 1 Corinthians 13:4-8 (NRSV). So the church aspires to proclaim a love that is rarely acquired. Only when we are perfected in heaven will we completely embody the love of Christ. Until then, we are merely learners, not perfected practitioners.

Who is our neighbor? In the Gospel of Luke 10:30-37, Jesus tells the story of the Good Samaritan to illustrate what it means to be a neighbor. The person who needs mercy is our neighbor. And he specifically uses the example of a person of a different religion who was despised by his audience to make his point. To follow Jesus is to show compassion, and that means doing what needs to be done. Showing mercy is getting messy and taking chances with a stranger. Jesus asks us to love the person we are with.

What about loving yourself? Are followers of Jesus supposed to love themselves? We can only give love because God loved us first. When we know the love of God, we are desperate to share that love. One has to love themself to give love. If you have a relationship with God, you know you are loved more than it is humanly possible to know love. If God loves us beyond our imagination, then how can we despise ourselves? We must love everything that is Christ-like in ourselves. We can also despise those attributes in ourselves that are not Christ-like. So we love the good that is in us. We despise that which is opposed to God. We love the hope, joy, faith, and peace we find in ourselves. One cannot share love if one is incapable of receiving love. One cannot be an instrument of God's love without having love to share. "We love because he first loved us," 1 John 4:19 (NRSV). That is the source and reason for our love because we are loved. We are commanded to love ourselves by accepting the love of God. When we receive the love of God, we know we are truly loveable.

Jesus Created the Church

The church was commissioned by Jesus. "And Jesus came and said to them, 'All authority in heaven and on earth has been given to me. Go therefore and make disciples of all nations, baptizing them in the name of the Father and of the Son and of the Holy Spirit, and teaching them to obey everything that I have commanded you. And remember, I am with you always, to the end of the age,'" Matthew 28:18-20 (NRSV). The church was and is sent out into the world to make disciples, baptize, and teach under the guidance of Jesus. A church that ceases to go out into the world is no longer under the leadership of Jesus. As Jesus and his disciples were sent out into the world to share the good news, so are we commissioned to do the same. It is not necessary whether the church goes out to its community or to another country. The response to the "great commission" of going out to serve Jesus is what matters. Every mature Christian is a minister. Every mature Christian is a missionary for Christ. Every mature Christian is an evangelist.

The Sacraments of Baptism and Communion

In the Gospels, there are two sacraments that Jesus instituted that have greater significance than all other sacraments. They are Baptism and Holy Communion. Jesus instituted these two sacraments which draw us closer to him and give us the opportunity to receive his Spirit. Through the elemental symbols of water, bread, and wine, we are involved in a supernatural event beyond our recognition. A spiritual transformation takes place in the sacramental act. This is why they are called sacred acts.

In Baptism, a person is incorporated into the church and the church receives its new member. The Baptism is also a sign and seal of the work of the Holy Spirit dwelling within the life of the individual. Baptism is a public profession of faith in God, Jesus Christ, and the Holy Spirit as the one God. Baptism is a renunciation of evil. Baptism is the death of the life enslaved to sin, and resurrection into life in Jesus Christ. Baptism is to know the reality of the forgiveness and mercy of God. Baptism is the sign and sealing of the beginning of the lifelong process of discipleship and sanctification in Jesus Christ.

Holy Communion is on its surface is a signifier of the reception of the Spirit of Christ by the individual and the unity of the Body of Christ in the participation of this sacrament. It is also a supernatural event where through these simple elements of bread and wine, the body and blood of Jesus Christ become our body and blood. "Then he took a loaf of bread, and when he had given thanks, he broke it and gave it to them, saying, 'This is my body, which is given for you. Do this in remembrance of me.' And he did the same with the cup after supper, saying, 'This cup that is poured out for you is the new covenant in my blood,'" Luke 22:19-20 (NRSV). We are called to the table to remember, receive, and reveal to the world Jesus in our lives.

The Enemy of the Church
The church has a supernatural enemy who hates the church and what it represents above all else. The enemy tried to destroy the church by persecution and killing its members for several hundred years and has continued that tactic in parts of the world to the present day. There are thousands of martyrs even today. This has had often the reverse effect of increasing the church. The more successful strategy for destroying the church has been internal attacks. By internal misdirection, corruption, and ossification, the church has been more successfully defeated.

The attacks on the church, whether covert or overt, are attacks on the Body of Christ and attacks on the person of Jesus. When Jesus was alive, he was verbally and physically attacked by the enemy. This persecution continues unabated to this day. The enemies of Jesus have become more sophisticated and subtle over time. Their motivation is the same. One of the most important lessons we have to learn in this life experience is discernment between good and evil.

There is a way to discern the difference between what is from God and what is opposed to God. Firstly, we have to use the four Gospels to determine if something is consistent with the life and teachings of Jesus. If it is consistent with the Jesus of the Gospels, then it is probably on the right path. If it is untypical of the actions and teachings of Jesus, then it is highly suspect. Secondly, we pray for divine guidance about the situation. Lay the dilemma out to God and ask for a sign to solve the problem. The sign will come when we are ready to receive it. This type of prayer will always be answered. We must we open to receive the answer. Thirdly, we consult with mature Christians about the situation. Presumably, there are pastors available for us to consult with on this sort of problem. This is another important role of the church in providing educated and ordained persons for spiritual direction and discernment. By consulting the Gospels, petitioning prayer, and spiritual direction, we can discern good from evil. We desperately need the community of the church to stay on the path of righteousness.

The Community
The Church of Jesus Christ provides us with community. Having a sense of community has always been critical to humans because we are social beings. As the world becomes more urbanized, we have increasingly lost our sense of community. In the urban environment, we become strangers without connection. Following Christ is entirely about relationships. Estrangement from our brothers and sisters is antithetical to the way of Jesus. The church must build a sense of community for all its members. The church has to assimilate new persons into the community to build the Body of Christ. Too often, the church has become exclusive and is blind to the numerous discreet ways that new people are excluded. The church must be inclusive of all sinners, which would be everyone. There must not be anyone excluded from the church. The church must never be a club of self-proclaimed righteous members only.

The church is not a building; rather, it is the congregation of people called by God to be the Body of Christ. When the focus of the church becomes maintaining the building, maintaining the social hierarchy of the members, and maintaining strict doctrinal correctness, the church is doomed. The Body of Christ is an organic living entity that has to adapt to change and do the painful work of spiritual growth. Too frequently, churches chose the way of death, but refuse to acknowledge their choice to die. Denial of its faults may be terminal.

The Way, The Truth, The Life

As Jesus is life and all that it entails, so must the Body of Christ be alive. This is creativity responding to worship, mission, and evangelism. Jesus was the ultimate artist of life, relating to every given situation that was so unique, authentic, and original that people did not know what to make of him. As the guiding Spirit of Christ leads the church, so must the church astonish the world. This doesn't sound like the church of the developed world today. Much of the present church presents itself as a museum. Where are the rules of liturgy in the Christian testaments? Other than a few references to proper decorum, there are no rules. Have we created an idolatry of stagnating worship?

To the millions in the developed world, who desperately need the love of God, the church of Jesus Christ appears dead and irrelevant. In the developing world, the church has more vitality because the power of convention has always dominated. In the growing edge of the church, there is creative worship, systematic mission, and unceasing evangelism. The flourishing church is the living Body of Christ.

May the Body of Christ reclaim the enthusiasm of the Spirit of Christ? As Jesus was lively, creative, profoundly truthful, and demanding of followers, so should the church be. Shall the church once again be the nurturing mother of creative expression in the arts as it once was? Music, art, poetry, and theatre once thrived in the church. Can the church reinvent itself in the image of Jesus Christ? The way of Jesus is going out into the world, reaching out to all people, and risking love. The way of Jesus is not conventional or safe. The way of Jesus is to "do nothing from selfish ambition or conceit, but in humility regard others as better than yourselves. Let each of you look not to your own interests, but to the interests of others. Let the same mind be in you that was in Christ Jesus," Philippians 2:3-5 (NRSV). Does the church have to die to be reborn? Is there no room in the church for radical followers of Jesus?

The truth of Jesus is the sole reason for the existence of the church. The church is responsible to proclaim that truth every time it meets and in everything it publishes. God sent Jesus to reveal to us the true nature of God and in this way done completely and definitively in the life, ministry, suffering, death, and resurrection of Jesus. The Holy Spirit is the Spirit of Truth that leads us and reveals Jesus to us. The church is God's instrument to lead all people to Jesus. This is the most important and non-negotiable purpose of the church. How often is the church timid or silent on issues to avoid controversy? People argue tirelessly about the color of paint to decorate the church building; meanwhile, injustice is rampant in our society.

Jesus established the church to help us be his instrument of reconciliation to God for all people. Because of human deficiencies, the church is far from the perfection of Jesus Christ. The church has been the best and, on a few occasions, the worst of human achievement. But what is the alternative? Most often, the church is a beacon of light in a world of darkness and shadows. Without the church, the world would be unbearably brutal, consistently cruel and always evil, and worse than the Roman Empire the church was born into.

Gifts in The Body of Christ

The church is the Body of Christ and the members of the church are to embody the Spirit of Christ. Each person in the church has been called by the Holy Spirit to have an important role in the work of the church and in the building up of the church. Every member of the church is given a gift or several gifts to equip them to do ministry in the church. Individually, the members of the church can do very little but collectively, there's very little that they cannot do. Through the power of the Holy Spirit, the church makes miracles happen every day.

Because human beings are imperfect, they bring their imperfections into the church, but the church must always strive to be the perfect embodiment of Jesus Christ. There is an old saying, "If you find the perfect church, don't go there, because it will no longer be perfect." Since we're all imperfect, we have to settle for the best of that we can do, given the talents and materials that we have to work with. Considering that every person in the church is unique and at a different stage of development in their spiritual journey, the church has to have a wide range of opportunities for people to grow in their faith and to Christian ministry. In order for the church to grow, it has to be an inviting environment, not an intimidating environment. The church must make the sinner and the stranger feel welcome because these are exactly the people that Jesus wants in his church, so that they may come to know him and be freed from their sin. So the church has to struggle with what appears to be a contradiction of saints loving sinners. The church is a place where people are to grow in holiness, and it is a place that invites and welcomes the unwashed sinner. Before we judge too quickly, only God truly knows who the saints are and who the sinners are. The church is a hospital for sinners and not a museum of saints.

The church cannot be all things to all people because it must obey the Commandment to love God with all your heart, mind, and strength, and to love your neighbor as yourself. Further, the church must always proclaim Jesus Christ as Lord and Savior. When a church puts anything or anyone above Jesus Christ, it is no longer a Christian church. Jesus is the way, the truth, and the life, and there can be no deviation from this and still be a Christian church. So the church must constantly be compared to Jesus Christ as he is revealed in the Bible and most especially in the Gospels. The person of Jesus and what he thought is the supreme authority for the Christian church. The Holy Spirit will lead us into the way, truth, and life of Jesus Christ.

The hidden danger is that, too often, people are influenced by unholy spirits and claim it to be the Holy Spirit thereby misleading the church. The Holy Spirit, which is the Spirit of Christ, cannot possibly be inconsistent with Jesus who is depicted in the Gospels. The Gospels of Matthew, Mark, Luke, and John were given to us by the Holy Spirit so that we would know Jesus. The Gospels are the reality check and the most useful tool for spiritual discernment. The Epistles were written after the life of Jesus by his disciples guided by the Holy Spirit for very specific circumstances in a time and culture extremely different than our own. To understand the Epistles, one has to understand the context and circumstances in which they were written. To remove them from their context and apply them literally to contemporary circumstances does them an injustice. The Epistles have a tremendous importance for the edification and inspiration of the Christian, but they can be misused by the ignorant. Everyone that comes into the church has their own personal agenda, but the agenda of the church must be to follow Jesus Christ faithfully. The church cannot allow itself to be deceived by human desires, ignorance, personal agendas, or deceiving spirits.

Another contradiction of the church is that it is to teach the morality of God and, at the same time, it is not to be the judge of souls. So how can the church be judgmental and nonjudgmental at the same time? For example, the church must teach the Ten Commandments because Jesus taught the Ten Commandments. If one investigated the background of the members of the church, one may find that every one of the Ten Commandments had been violated, some more than others. The church has to accept responsibility for its own sinfulness and confess its sin and ask for the forgiveness of God. The church, which is the members who constitute the church, must acknowledge sin openly and not be hypocrites pretending that they have achieved perfection. The Ten Commandments must be taught, and it must be acknowledged that they have been violated, and people must seek forgiveness for their sin. Jesus hated hypocrisy and this is dramatically demonstrated in several instances in the Gospels. When the church becomes hypocritical, it is no longer a friend of Jesus; rather, it has become his enemy. For the church to be what Jesus wanted it to be, it must be like the sinner who went to the temple to pray, acknowledged his sin, and asked God for mercy. It cannot be like the Pharisee who went to the temple to pray and proclaimed his own virtue. The church is composed of sinners and must confess its sinfulness, seeking God's forgiveness.

The church must be a place of compassion because Jesus was the very embodiment of compassion. People in the church should have compassion for each other and, even more importantly, have compassion for the whole world, especially the poor and afflicted. Jesus had a special compassion for the poor and needy, and so should his church. The church must always be looking beyond its own walls to minister to the poor and needy.

The great injustice in this world is the economic injustice of our global economics. A small percentage of the world's population enjoy tremendous wealth and opportunity while the majority of the population of this planet live in terrible poverty with little or no opportunity for work, health, shelter, or education. This may be the way of the world, but it is not the way of Jesus Christ. Jesus commands us to go out into the world and care for the poor and those who are oppressed. The fact that there are millions of people in the world who live in poverty and are exploited for the benefit of the wealthy minority of the population is the great injustice in the world today. Can the church be indifferent to the billions of people who have little or no education, health care, meaningful work, security, adequate shelter, or sufficient food? Christians can do something about this, and in the process make the most effective witness for Jesus and evangelize for Jesus Christ. Mission and evangelism are two sides of the same coin and need to be done together, just as Jesus taught and healed.

The Sign of the Kingdom

The church is a sign of the kingdom of God. The church is not the kingdom of God because the kingdom of God is not yet come, but it shows the way to the kingdom of God and what it may be like. The church is a place for the worship of God; it is a group of people engaged in mission and evangelism, and it is a congregation who love and support one another. The early Christian church grew at a phenomenal rate in spite of the fact that the Roman Empire did everything in its power to annihilate it. One of the main reasons for its success was the love and support that Christians had for each other. Their love for each other was extraordinary in contrast to the cruelty of Roman society. People were attracted to Christianity for the love that was exhibited within the Christian community. The world may appear to be more civilized today than it was in Roman times, but is not the cruelty just more subtle? Does the church stand out in the community as a unique place where people love and support each other? If the church is truly exhibiting to the world the love of Christ within the congregation, would not people want to be a part of it? The true success of the church is not how big it is, or how much money was spent on the facilities, or how many programs go on in the church. The true success of a church is how the congregation loves and supports one another, how they worship God in truth and in spirit, and how committed they are to mission and evangelism.

This world desperately needs the Christian Church today before we destroy this world. God has patience, but how much longer is God going to wait for humans to become the children of God behaving as such? The church is the only human instrument that can bring about the conversion of the world. If this were the focus of the church, the Holy Spirit would kindle a revival that would consume the entire planet. There is no doubt this is the will of God. We are either participating in God's plan or we are in defiance of God's plan. We pray, "Come Lord Jesus! Come!"

CHAPTER 4
THE PERSON OF JESUS

The essential understanding of the Christian faith is based on an appreciation of the incarnation of God in the person of Jesus. The intervention of God in human history through the incarnation of Jesus Christ was personal. God is capable of micro managing and macro managing the world simultaneously. Since human beings are not capable of this kind of multitasking, it is impossible for us to even imagine that capacity of God to care about us individually. Our relationship with God is extremely personal. The Psalmist wrote in Psalm 111:10 (NRSV), "The fear of the Lord is the beginning of wisdom." It is fearsome to know the extent to which God is intimately involved in our lives. God knows everything we think, feel, and do. In Luke 16:15 (NRSV), Jesus states, "God knows your hearts." Every moment and every experience of our lives is known to our Maker.

Fear, awe, and reverence are the only reasonable responses to the knowledge that we are intimately connected to our maker. Having a personal relationship with God is what God desires from us, and we can choose to accept this relationship or not. The delusion we are separated from God gives us a sense of freedom without responsibility. In Galatians 6:7 (NRSV), "God is not mocked, for you reap whatever you sow." Although we are free to act, we can never escape the responsibility for our actions. There is a law of physics that says for every action there is an equal but opposite reaction. In the spiritual world, there is a corresponding reaction to every action. Whether we are willing to take responsibility for our actions or not, we are completely and solely responsible for our actions. God has sent us teachers, prophets, and Jesus Christ to teach us how to be that children of God. God has sent his Holy Spirit to abide in our hearts and minds. We can be guided by the Spirit of Christ to become the people that God created us to be.

When we know Jesus, God is no longer a mystery. Because Jesus and God are one nature, to know the one is to know the other. Jesus said, "The Father and I are one," in John 10:30 (NRSV). What Jesus revealed about God is more than everything that we need to know about God. The more familiar we become with Jesus by studying the Bible, being a part of the Body of Christ, growing in a personal relationship through prayer, and serving in his name, the better we understand Jesus. The entire creation teaches us about the Creator but only the external nature of the Creator. It is through Jesus that we learned the heart and will of the Creator. In the revelation of Jesus Christ, we have an intimacy with God.

The Gospels of Matthew, Mark, Luke, and John are testimonies of faith from the first disciples of Jesus. These Gospels were written down in their present form by the first disciples or the close followers of the first disciples. Each Gospel differs according to the intentions and interests of the disciples who wrote them. The fact that each Gospel has its own character, and there are some discrepancies among each other, serves to enhance the veracity of these testimonies of faith. The Gospels were written so that others might believe that Jesus was the Christ. If, for example, different portrait artists paint the same subject, the differences in the portraits would be most striking. The Gospel writers were not trying to write strictly history or biography; they were giving a testimony about that revelation of God in Jesus Christ. The Gospel writers did not exaggerate or embellish what Jesus had done because they knew that they were responsible to God for every word they wrote. If anything, they minimized what Jesus did during his ministry in this world, since he had done so much more that was not recorded. In John 21:25 (NRSV), "But there are also many other things that Jesus did; if every one of them were written down, I suppose that the world itself could not contain the books that would be written." The Gospels were written so that you too might know the perfect revelation of God and Christ.

For us to identify with God, God chose to identify with us. In the birth narratives, we have the Divine Being conceived in the womb of the Virgin Mary. The DNA of Mary was mixed with a Divine DNA from God to create an individual that had never existed before and has never been duplicated. This child had all the frailty of a human and the capacity to be the vehicle for the Divine will of God. The mystery of the full divinity and full humanity of Jesus is one of the beautiful and effable revelations of the Christian faith.

What we know about Jesus' early life is his early circumstances. He was born into a poor family along with the overwhelming majority of the population of the world. His father Joseph worked as a carpenter/builder and his wages would have been about one or more denari a day. One denari would have brought a loaf of bread. The family probably kept a few modest animals and grew some of their own food. Mary would have contributed to the family through weaving and gardening. The male child would have entered the work force as soon as he was able to contribute to the family income. Jesus must have had the opportunity to study the Torah as a child in Nazareth because he was able to read Hebrew. Jesus may have been exposed to Greco Roman culture in Sepphoris which was a growing city near to Nazareth. There is a site in Nazareth that may be the very house Jesus grew up in. Their home probably consisted of two small rooms built partially into the hillside. There would be an open fire pit in the center of the house with little or no furniture. Any domestic animals stayed in the house at night. This was a simple subsistence life.

Since Nazareth was a small village of approximately two hundred to five hundred people, it is unlikely that there was sufficient work for Joseph there. Three miles away was a growing major city of Sepphoris, so it is most probable that Joseph and Jesus worked in this urban environment. Jesus would have encountered Greeks, Romans, Arabs, and many other people in addition to a wide range of Jewish people. In this city, there were many large beautiful homes with beautiful mosaic decorations. Many of these have been excavated and can be seen today. There was a large Greek amphitheater still intact. This city was a center of rabbinic study where Jesus could have studied and attended synagogue. The language of commerce and learning was Greek, the common language of the people was Aramaic, the language of the Roman government and army was Latin, the language of classical literature and philosophy was Greek, and the language of the synagogue was Hebrew. Many people spoke several languages and it would have been typical for a man of Jesus' time to become multilingual. In the Gospels, there are examples of him using Greek, Aramaic, and Hebrew.

According to Luke 2:40 (NRSV), "The child grew and became strong, filled with wisdom; and the favor of God was upon him." For Jesus to have the human experience, he would have to learn just as we do. Apparently, his childhood was so normal that only one event is preserved during this time. In Luke 2:41-43 (NRSV), "Now every year his parents went to Jerusalem for the festival of the Passover. And when he was twelve years old, they went up as usual for the festival. When the festival was ended and they started to return, the boy Jesus stayed behind in Jerusalem, but his parents did not know it." This informs us that Joseph and Mary were observant Jews and took the time and expense to go to Jerusalem for Passover. Jerusalem would have been mobbed with tens of thousands of visitors from all over the Roman Empire for the great festival of Passover. They were not obligated to make this pilgrimage, but the pious came for this occasion as often as possible. For Joseph and Mary, this journey from Nazareth would take several days of walking each way. There were expenses of travel and the loss of wages so it was a big sacrifice for a poor family.

We learn that at the age of twelve, Jesus was treated as a mature person because he could be independent of his parents enough that they did not miss him on their departure from Jerusalem, assuming that he had joined the group of travelers. Apparently, he behaved in a very mature manner for his age. In Luke 2:44-47 (NRSV), "Assuming that he was in the group of travelers, they went a day's journey. Then they started to look for him among their relatives and friends. When they did not find him, they returned to Jerusalem to search for him. After three days they found him in the temple, sitting among the teachers, listening to them and asking them questions. And all who heard him were amazed at his understanding and his answers." In order for Jesus to have the human experience, he would have come into this world like a human child without knowledge, and over time gained knowledge and wisdom as any human being would. It is also easy to imagine that Jesus was extremely gifted and had intuitive abilities that we cannot begin to imagine. At the age of twelve, Jesus was at the temple in Jerusalem speaking with the rabbis and scholars in such a way that they were amazed by his understanding. Jesus was a child prodigy by his divine nature which was his birthright. He was fully human and fully divine.

Jesus was apparently so completely absorbed in his theological conversations in the temple that he neglected his parents, or perhaps he had the foresight to know that they would find him in the temple. When Mary and Joseph found him, they chastised him, but Jesus had a response which must have astonished them all the more. In Luke 2:48-50 (NRSV), "When his parents saw him they were astonished; and his mother said to him, 'Child, why have you treated us like this? Look, your father and I have been searching for you in great anxiety.' He said to them, 'Why were you searching for me? Did you not know that I must be in my Father's house?' But they did not understand what he said to them." Mary and Joseph had been given the greatest privilege and responsibility that any mother and father had ever been given, which was to raise the Son of God. Based on the success of Jesus' upbringing, they must have been the most wonderful parents. Certainly, God had chosen them because God knew that they would be the parents God wanted them to be. How difficult it must have been for them to keep up with this child prodigy, and to try to understand the mystery of the incarnation of the one who was fully human and fully divine. Raising this unique boy in a small village must have been extremely challenging.

Jesus was an obedient child and treated his parents with honor. Nazareth was a tiny and humble village, where everybody knew everybody else's business as is common in village life. Jesus grew up, behaved in humility, and found favor in a small community. Later in his life, when he came back as a man to this village to preach and teach them, they were unable to readjust to the Jesus who was the Christ because they remembered him as the "village boy" who was just like them. During his life, Jesus was just another man to the people that he'd grown up with because that's all they had ever known him to be growing up amongst them. Therefore, it can be assumed that he did not perform any miracles or healings prior to the beginning of his ministry that began after his baptism later in life.

We read in Luke 2:51-52 (NRSV), "Then he went down with them and came to Nazareth, and was obedient to them. His mother treasured all these things in her heart. And Jesus increased in wisdom and in years, and in divine and human favor." Since it was God's intention to completely identify with the human condition, it must have been gratifying to God to see Jesus flourish in his humanity without relying upon his divine abilities. How did Jesus struggle with his divinity and his humanity during these years of preparation for his mission to be Savior of the world?

When Jesus was approximately 30 years old, he set out to begin his ministry by seeking John the Baptist so that he might be baptized by John. We do not know if they had a relationship before this time, but it is quite likely that they did since they were cousins. John the Baptist was reluctant to baptize Jesus because he knew that he was the Messiah, but Jesus wanted to establish the sacrament for his followers by establishing the precedent of baptism. When he was baptized, there was a voice from heaven that spoke to those present announcing that Jesus really was the Son of God. In Matthew 3:13-17 (NRSV), "Then Jesus came from Galilee to John at the Jordan, to be baptized by him. John would have prevented him, saying, 'I need to be baptized by you, and do you come to me?' But Jesus answered him, 'Let it be so now; for it is proper for us in this way to fulfill all righteousness.' Then he consented. And when Jesus had been baptized, just as he came up from the water, suddenly the heavens were opened to him and he saw the Spirit of God descending like a dove and alighting on him. And a voice from heaven said, 'This is my Son, the Beloved, with whom I am well pleased.'" This voice may have been heard by many people because it was not long after this incident when Jesus began calling his disciples and they joined him without reservation. It is possible the word had spread about the voice of God speaking at the baptism of Jesus. Since the expectation for the coming of the Messiah was very high already, this may have been the sign that some people were looking for and ready to believe. It is quite likely that a number of Jesus' early disciples had been followers of John the Baptist first. After the incident of the voice of God speaking, many turned their allegiance to Jesus with the encouragement of John the Baptist.

Before beginning his ministry, Jesus subjected himself to an ordeal of prayer and fasting in the desert. He did this to clarify his understanding of what his ministry would be, and to perfect his communication with God. It was the Spirit of God that led him into the wilderness so that they might converse with one another.

During this time of prayer and fasting, Jesus was tempted by the evil one. There were three temptations offered to Jesus, which represent three of the primary ways in which we are tempted.

Firstly, the evil one commanded Jesus to turn stone into bread as proof of his divinity. Jesus had been fasting for very long time and was ravenously hungry, but he refused to use his power for his own gain. And he did not have to prove who he was to the evil one. How are we constantly tempted by material things in our desire to have more and more? We spend our lives chasing after food, clothes, cars, houses, money, and status symbols. Do we not constantly try to prove our worth to other people? We even go to the point of making fools ourselves because of our lack of self-awareness of who we really are.

Secondly, the evil one offered Jesus power over the whole world if Jesus would only worship him. The desire for the ability to dominate people has driven this world into countless and unspeakable evils. Jesus had no desire for worldly power and had no need to dominate people. Jesus would never forsake the love of God by worshiping anything other than God, and Jesus would never worship the evil one. We constantly create idols in the hopes that we will gain powers and domination we crave. God expressly forbids us to have any god or idol before us except the one true God. What are the false gods we worship?

Thirdly, the evil one commands Jesus to put God to the test by throwing himself off the highest point of the temple and commanding the Angels to rescue him from the fall. God does not test us. God allows us to be tested and tempted in this world, but we are not to put God to the test. God does not have to prove God to us. If we love God, our faith and love of God is sufficient.

The Scripture is in Luke 4:1-15 (NRSV), "Jesus, full of the Holy Spirit, returned from the Jordan and was led by the Spirit in the wilderness, where for forty days he was tempted by the devil. He ate nothing at all during those days, and when they were over, he was famished. The devil said to him, 'If you are the Son of God, command this stone to become a loaf of bread.' Jesus answered him, 'It is written, "One does not live by bread alone."' Then the devil led him up and showed him in an instant all the kingdoms of the world. And the devil said to him, 'To you I will give their glory and all this authority; for it has been given over to me, and I give it to anyone I please. If you, then, will worship me, it will all be yours.' Jesus answered him, 'It is written, "Worship the Lord your God, and serve only him."' Then the devil took him to Jerusalem, and placed him on the pinnacle of the temple, saying to him, 'If you are the Son of God, throw yourself down from here, for it is written, "He will command his angels concerning you, to protect you," and "On their hands they will bear you up, so that you will not dash your foot against a stone."' Jesus answered him, 'It is said, "Do not put the Lord your God to the test."' When the devil had finished every test, he departed from him until an opportune time. Then Jesus, filled with the power of the Spirit, returned to Galilee, and a report about him spread through all the surrounding country. He began to teach in their synagogues and was praised by everyone."

Jesus has many titles such as Friend, Messiah, Christ, Savior, King of Kings, and Lord. Each describes a facet of his identity. Consider Jesus as our brother. In fact, he is closer to us than any human brother could possibly be, because he knows us better than we know ourselves, and he loves us more than we can ever love another person. Jesus came into this world to bring us into the family of God. We are no longer strangers to God.

Read Mark 3:34-35 (NRSV), "And looking at those who sat around him, he said, 'Here are my mother and my brothers! Whoever does the will of God is my brother and sister and mother.'" To believe and follow Jesus unites us in intimacy, by the indwelling Holy Spirit, to the Holy Family of God. To really know Jesus is having a relationship with him that is more intimate than a familial relation.

Jesus had the power over the forces of nature and he used those powers to increase the faith of his disciples. Jesus was so intimately connected to God that he could have done anything that he wanted, but there are recorded a few instances where he used this power.

Jesus does not want us to believe in him through demonstrations of power, magic, or coercion. We may be initially attracted to the miracles, but the deeper attraction is his heart of love. Jesus wants us to receive his love and to return his love with our love. Our love is demonstrated in our faith and obedience to him.

Mark 4:37-41 (NRSV), "A great windstorm arose, and the waves beat into the boat, so that the boat was already being swamped. But he was in the stern, asleep on the cushion; and they woke him up and said to him, 'Teacher, do you not care that we are perishing?' He woke up and rebuked the wind, and said to the sea, 'Peace! Be still!' Then the wind ceased, and there was a dead calm. He said to them, 'Why are you afraid? Have you still no faith?' And they were filled with great awe and said to one another, 'Who then is this, that even the wind and the sea obey him?'" This is but one example of Jesus' God-like power.

Jesus held nothing back from his disciples. He promised to them the good things that were going to happen to them, and he warned them of the bad things that lay ahead. There are many instances in the Gospels where he told his disciples about his suffering and death in Jerusalem, but they refused to believe him concerning these things. Jesus warns us about the consequences of our actions, but do we take seriously what he has told us? Jesus is completely honest with us and desires honesty in return.

In Matthew 16:21 (NRSV), "From that time on, Jesus began to show his disciples that he must go to Jerusalem and undergo great suffering at the hands of the elders and chief priests and scribes, and be killed, and on the third day be raised."

To strengthen the faith of three of his disciples, Jesus took them up to the top of the mountain and showed them who he really was. He did this to strengthen their faith because he was coming to the end of his ministry, and this was the time for them to begin their ministry. On this mountaintop, they were given the vision of Jesus with Elijah and Moses and his full glory. He appeared to them with brilliance that was brighter than lightening. These disciples needed to know who Jesus really was and he showed them the light of God. The disciples wanted to enshrine the experience, but Jesus would not allow that and told them to keep it secret for a while. When we have a supernatural experience of who Jesus really is, does it empower us to go out in ministry to the world?

Read Luke 9:28-36, "Now about eight days after these sayings Jesus took with him Peter and John and James, and went up on the mountain to pray. And while he was praying, the appearance of his face changed, and his clothes became dazzling white. Suddenly they saw two men, Moses and Elijah, talking to him. They appeared in glory and were speaking of his departure, which he was about to accomplish at Jerusalem. Now Peter and his companions were weighed down with sleep; but since they had stayed awake, they saw his glory and the two men who stood with him. Just as they were leaving him, Peter said to Jesus, 'Master, it is good for us to be here; let us make three dwellings, one for you, one for Moses, and one for Elijah'—not knowing what he said. While he was saying this, a cloud came and overshadowed them; and they were terrified as they entered the cloud. Then from the cloud came a voice that said, 'This is my Son, my Chosen; listen to him!' When the voice had spoken, Jesus was found alone. And they kept silent and in those days told no one any of the things they had seen."

Jesus had the human emotions that you and I do. There are two recorded occasions recorded in the Gospel where Jesus weeps. One occasion is when he hears the news of the death of his friend Lazarus, and the second is when he weeps for Jerusalem. Jesus weeps for us because he came into this world to bring us his peace and love and instead we have rejected him and chosen strife and war instead. Jesus weeps for us because he empathizes with our suffering. Jesus did not come to the world to bring an end to suffering, but he did come to strengthen, comfort, and heal those who suffer. "Blessed are those who mourn, for they shall be comforted," Matthew 5:4 (NRSV).

In Luke 19:41-44 (NRSV), "As he came near and saw the city, he wept over it, saying, 'If you, even you, had only recognized on this day the things that make for peace! But now they are hidden from your eyes. Indeed, the days will come upon you, when your enemies will set up ramparts around you and surround you, and hem you in on every side. They will crush you to the ground, you and your children within you, and they will not leave within you one stone upon another; because you did not recognize the time of your visitation from God.'"

Jesus sometimes used forceful action and was very aggressive. In his outrage at the corruption in the temple in Jerusalem of the money changers and the sellers of animals for sacrifice, he physically attacked these practices which desecrated the sacred place of worship. When he did this, he won the enmity of the corrupt priests of the temple who profited from the system of exchanging money and selling sacrificial animals. Jesus is often portrayed as meek and mild, but this is an incomplete understanding of the true Jesus of the Gospels. Jesus could be very forceful and assertive when it was necessary. Do we emasculate Jesus in order to keep him from being a threat to our corrupt society? Do we nullify the power of the Holy Spirit in order to avoid the risk of creating enemies?

In Matthew 21:10-16 (NRSV), "When he entered Jerusalem, the whole city was in turmoil, asking, 'Who is this?' The crowds were saying, 'This is the prophet Jesus from Nazareth in Galilee.' Then Jesus entered the temple and drove out all who were selling and buying in the temple, and he overturned the tables of the money changers and the seats of those who sold doves. He said to them, 'It is written, "My house shall be called a house of prayer"; but you are making it a den of robbers.' The blind and the lame came to him in the temple, and he cured them. But when the chief priests and the scribes saw the amazing things that he did, and heard the children crying out in the temple, 'Hosanna to the Son of David,' they became angry and said to him, 'Do you hear what these are saying?' Jesus said to them, 'Yes; have you never read, "Out of the mouths of infants and nursing babies you have prepared praise for yourself"?'" Jesus caused a huge disruption in the Temple, cleansing it of commerce. Many scholars believe this directly led to his crucifixion.

Jesus gives us in his teaching and by example a clear understanding of what it means to be his disciple. We are to serve one another as he served us. In the kingdom of God, there is no hierarchy of importance. Even though each of us has been given unique gifts and abilities, we are all equal in the Body of Christ.

Jesus gives us a perfect example of what a true child of must be like. God in human form served in the traditional role of a slave, washing the feet of his disciples. The humble servant is the model of Christ-like love. How opposite is this simplicity compared to the worldly grandeur and excesses of wealth and power of our rulers. Jesus challenges our common illusions about privilege. The role of a servant is the highest office in the Kingdom of God.

In John 13:1-15 (NRSV), "Now before the festival of the Passover, Jesus knew that his hour had come to depart from this world and go to the Father. Having loved his own who were in the world, he loved them to the end. The devil had already put it into the heart of Judas son of Simon Iscariot to betray him. And during supper Jesus, knowing that the Father had given all things into his hands, and that he had come from God and was going to God, got up from the table, took off his outer robe, and tied a towel around himself. Then he poured water into a basin and began to wash the disciples' feet and to wipe them with the towel that was tied around him. He came to Simon Peter, who said to him, 'Lord, are you going to wash my feet?' Jesus answered, 'You do not know now what I am doing, but later you will understand.' Peter said to him, 'You will never wash my feet.' Jesus answered, 'Unless I wash you, you have no share with me.' Simon Peter said to him, 'Lord, not my feet only but also my hands and my head!' Jesus said to him,

'One who has bathed does not need to wash, except for the feet, but is entirely clean. And you are clean, though not all of you.' For he knew who was to betray him; for this reason he said, 'Not all of you are clean.' After he had washed their feet, had put on his robe, and had returned to the table, he said to them, 'Do you know what I have done to you? You call me Teacher and Lord—and you are right, for that is what I am. So if I, your Lord and Teacher, have washed your feet, you also ought to wash one another's feet. For I have set you an example, that you also should do as I have done to you.'"

One of the most difficult challenges in following Jesus is to be a humble servant as Jesus was. These humble servants of Christ are all around us, often unrecognized. They may be a grandparent, a neighbor, a person washing the dishes in the church, the housekeeper in the hospital, the wise mechanic, a teacher, the server at the restaurant, or any of a thousand vocations. Notice them and encourage them. They need a little love and respect too.

The Gospels have numerous examples of the character and person of Jesus. These few examples illustrate some of what we can know about him from the people who knew him best. Study of the Gospels is the direct knowledge of God. The Gospels give us standards by which to evaluate all other scripture and doctrine.

The person of Jesus from my personal experience

Jesus is God. God has revealed God's heart and will in human form in the person of Jesus. We may know God and have an intimate relationship with God through Jesus.

When I was a child, I learned in church about Jesus, but I hardly knew him as a living person. As a child, I trusted what I learned, but this knowledge is mostly superficial compared to knowing the person and having a strong connection to that person. When I had my near death experience at the age of thirty-eight, I met Jesus in person and began to know him as a person. Ever since, he has been the most important thing in my life and I hope to serve him in all that I do.

The immediate experience of meeting Jesus is one of awe, reverence, ecstasy, and fear all simultaneously. If there had been a rock to hide behind, I would have hid because of my unworthiness. He came upon me, touched me, healed me, embraced me, and filled me with indescribable love. This changed everything about my life forever. My life is dedicated to sharing this love with the entire world. I desperately want everyone to know the love of Jesus for themselves. There is a sense of urgency about this work. Jesus is closer to us than we are to ourselves, and he is eager to be known. Millions of people over thousands of years have had the exquisite opportunity to meet Jesus and receive his love. Knowing Jesus is very different than knowing about Jesus. The love of Jesus present in your heart, mind, and spirit changes everything in your life. When you have this great love, you want to live a life pleasing to him.

The difficulty with attempting to communicate the love of Jesus is our language is incapable to describe that love. If we compiled all the superlatives together to describe his love, they would be inadequate. The best we can do is describe our reaction to that love. What is the impact of that love on our life?

"Amazing Grace" is a well-known hymn to Christians that many relate to as describing what knowing Jesus is like. I did not know this hymn before my conversion, and after my conversion I heard this hymn, and I was emotionally overwhelmed. I couldn't stop crying for joy because it expressed perfectly what I was feeling. Thirty years later, every time I hear "Amazing Grace," it rocks me to the core of my being. It eloquently and simply says it all.

The comparison between Jesus' love and our love is so extreme as to be preposterous. Human love is barely comparable to the greatness of Jesus' love. His love is so vast it would be unbearable except it is a love that affirms and supports the individual. The holiness of God is so beyond any sense a person may of have of their holiness; they are not comparable, but we strive to be holy as God is holy. God is the Creator and we are the creature and we were created to be in relationship with our creator. The appropriate response to our situation is to return the love and be obedient to the revealed commandments as best we can. God's love enhances or life, gives us a peace that surpasses all understanding, and fills us with an abiding joy. This love once experienced becomes the foundation of our existence.

God wants us to become the person we were created to be before we were born. God desires us to fulfill our potential as a child of God. God's grace is an affirmation of us as individual persons made uniquely with qualities of the divine. When I met Jesus, it was immediately evident that he knew me better than I knew myself and that he liked me as a friend. In fact, he is the best friend anyone could ever have. He wants only the best for us. He always tells us the truth, even when we don't want to hear it. He showed me my life and shared his joy and sorrow with the way that I had lived and the choices I had made. There were a multitude of instances where my actions disappointed him, disturbed him, and upset him. These were my sins and I was so ashamed at how much these sins hurt my best friend. He was completely honest with me and I had no excuses. There were many times when I begged him to stop showing me my past life. He told me repeatedly that it was necessary and we continued. The truth was the judgment of my life and there was no evasion possible. During this explicit disclosure of my life, he constantly shared his love for me. Without this support of love, my life review would have been unbearable. Jesus loved me, he liked me, and he hated my sin. Sin is the barrier to having a relationship with God. I had ignored God, rebelled against God, and denied God with my sin. My desire was to satisfy my desires and be independent of God so that I could do what I wanted. Does this sound familiar?

This sin goes back to the beginning of humankind with Adam and Eve. Humans lived in blissful ignorance until they used their free will to choose awareness of good and evil. They disobeyed God and were filled with shame. They alienated themselves from God and lost innocence and paradise. We are free to choose and we have the ability to make the right choices or not. When we choose to be our own god, we separate ourselves from the only true God. This grieves God and God seeks reconciliation. Ultimately this alienation from God has consequences in this world and in the afterlife.

God gave me a great gift which was to see and feel the consequences of my actions. Our choices determine our fate. God allows us to choose between heaven and hell by our every thought, word, and deed. God gives us unlimited opportunities to repent and be forgiven. God, in the person of Jesus, even suffered and died for our forgiveness. God forces no one to heaven or hell. We are responsible for those outcomes. God passionately desires all people would seek heaven, and God grieves when people turn from God. Sadly, many people turn from God. They go to a place where they can try to gratify all their desires but they are never gratified. Their existence is torment. The physical suffering of hell is minor in relation to the emotional torment. The spirit is on fire.

Jesus came to rescue all of humankind. The response has not been what it needs to be. In so many ways we have not been faithful servants that bring our sisters and brothers to the Savior. The enemies of God have been highly effective in deception about life and God's will for humanity. Jesus wants a worldwide conversion now. Jesus stressed to me the urgency for this revival and conversion immediately. Jesus is eager for as many souls as possible to come home to heaven. Jesus weeps for every soul that rejects God and goes to hell. Jesus loves us and wants us to live in the bliss of heaven with God and all the saints.

The love Jesus gives us is beyond description. There is more to his love that is equally important to share. Jesus Christ, who is the creative activity of God, created us. He really likes his creatures.

We are created in every detail by him and he is extremely fond of us as we are. In the eyes of Jesus, each of us is unique, important, and beautiful. The only thing he does not like about us is when we destroy the goodness in ourselves or in others. We were created to glorify God in this life and in heaven. It pleases Jesus when we live lives doing our best to please God and it saddens Jesus when we make little or no effort to glorify God. Each of us has a purpose unique to our individual gifts and abilities, and these were given us to be a light to the world. We are to let our light shine in the darkness just as Jesus did.

Jesus feels our emotions and our thoughts. Surprisingly, Jesus has the best sense of humor and playfulness. He is a joy to be with. Too often, our image of Jesus is of a strict authority figure watching to see if we will make a mistake so we may be condemned. This is completely false image of Jesus. Jesus is kind, patient, funny, and compassionate. He is our best friend and really likes us just the way we are. Of course he likes us the way we are because He made us just as we are. He wants us to blossom into beautiful beings and glorify God. It is important to remember that he lived in this world as a human and completely gets the human condition. All of our mistakes are learning opportunities. All of our joys make Jesus smile. He knows our pain and suffers with us. One could not ask for a better friend. This is the Jesus that everyone needs to know. This little life of ours is a great gift to participate in the ever-expanding creation to the infinite expression of God's love.

CHAPTER 5

THE PASSION

The death and resurrection of Jesus Christ is the singular most important event in the history of humankind. The Gospels tell these events in detail, so I will use the Gospels to tell the story and make comments after each selection. To understand the passion is the key to understanding the purpose of the incarnation. These events were written down by witnesses or told by witnesses to the men who wrote them down. The small variations are based on the different perspectives of the individual witnesses.

Jesus loved life. He did not want to die and he did not want to suffer a horrible death. He allowed the people that he loved to torture and kill him out of obedience to God's will. Jesus died for us to accomplish our salvation. His death gave us eternal life in several ways. When Jesus came into this world, he took upon himself our human nature and, in his self-identification with us, he took upon himself the full human experience, including suffering and death. By his resurrection from death, he showed us that we could be resurrected from death through our faith in him. Human beings are not immortal and can only become immortal by the grace of God. Jesus Christ showed to us his victory over death. Jesus also conquered the power of sin. Sin and death no longer controlled human destiny. Through his sacrifice, our sins are forgiven, and when we accept Jesus as our Savior we are no longer slaves to the power of sin. In the old days of Judaism, animals were sacrificed to expiate the sins of people. Jesus gave himself as the final and complete sacrifice for all human sin. His death was the atonement and redemption so we could now approach God having been justified by Jesus. Our sins were paid for by his blood.

The greatest fear that human beings have is the fear of death. Through our faith in Jesus Christ, we no longer have to fear death because we know that we will be raised up to heaven and be made perfect through Jesus. We no longer have to fear suffering because he suffered for us, and he is with us in our suffering, giving us the strength to bear anything. We can offer our suffering up to him as our small sacrifice as he suffered and redeemed us.

When Jesus went to Jerusalem and made his triumphal entry into the city, cleansed the temple, and taught openly on the temple steps, he knew the terrible consequences of his actions. He had been planning for this culmination of his ministry for several years and knew exactly what was going to happen. He was executed in the most demeaning and painful way that the Roman Empire reserved for the worst criminals. To die on the cross was the most shameful death imaginable. The pain, emotionally and physically, was excruciating. Before he was executed, he was flogged almost to the point of death. During his trial and up to the point of his death, he was spat upon, viciously mocked, struck in the face, and demeaned in every cruel way possible. His sacrifice took him to a point of humiliation that few people have ever experienced. He suffered all of this so that we might have life. This happened to a man who was without sin and embodied the divine love of God.

In the Garden of Gethsemane

In Mark 14:32-42 (NRSV), "They went to a place called Gethsemane; and he said to his disciples, 'Sit here while I pray.' He took with him Peter and James and John, and began to be distressed and agitated. And he said to them, 'I am deeply grieved, even to death; remain here, and keep awake.' And going a little farther, he threw himself on the ground and prayed that, if it were possible, the hour might pass from him. He said, 'Abba, Father, for you all things are possible; remove this cup from me; yet, not what I want, but what you want.' He came and found them sleeping; and he said to Peter, 'Simon, are you asleep? Could you not keep awake one hour? Keep awake and pray that you may not come into the time of trial; the spirit indeed is willing, but the flesh is weak.' And again he went away and prayed, saying the same words. And once more he came and found them sleeping, for their eyes were very heavy; and they did not know what to say to him. He came a third time and said to them, 'Are you still sleeping and taking your rest? Enough! The hour has come; the Son of Man is betrayed into the hands of sinners. Get up, let us be going. See, my betrayer is at hand.'"

Jesus knew the horror that awaited him and he chose to spend his last few hours of freedom in the company of his disciples. These men who had followed him faithfully for several years appear to be clueless about what was going to happen to him, even though he had told them repeatedly exactly what lay ahead. As he prayed and contemplated what lay before him, he was in torment. He suffered alone because his disciples fell asleep rather than giving him the comfort of their company and their prayers. How we betray him, intentionally and unintentionally, has not changed in two thousand years. Every one of us participates in some way in the suffering and death of Jesus. If we think we are somehow better than the disciples who loved him, we deceive ourselves. During this ordeal, Jesus was alone, deserted by his disciples. We are never alone in our trials because he is always with us.

The Arrest of Jesus
In Mark 14:43-52 (NRSV), "Immediately, while he was still speaking, Judas, one of the twelve, arrived; and with him there was a

crowd with swords and clubs, from the chief priests, the scribes, and the elders. Now the betrayer had given them a sign, saying, 'The one I will kiss is the man; arrest him and lead him away under guard.' So when he came, he went up to him at once and said, 'Rabbi!' and kissed him. Then they laid hands on him and arrested him. But one of those who stood near drew his sword and struck the slave of the high priest, cutting off his ear. Then Jesus said to them, 'Have you come out with swords and clubs to arrest me as though I were a bandit? Day after day I was with you in the temple teaching, and you did not arrest me. But let the scriptures be fulfilled.' All of them deserted him and fled. A certain young man was following him, wearing nothing but a linen cloth. They caught hold of him, but he left the linen cloth and ran off naked."

How appropriate that they came to arrest Jesus in the middle of the night. Since he had been teaching in the temple every day, they could have arrested him there. But they did not, because they were afraid of his followers, and they were children of the night. Their lives were enslaved to emotions of greed, shame, guilt, revenge, and jealousy. So they came with swords and clubs as if he were some dangerous criminal. There was relatively little resistance and his disciples ran away abandoning Jesus. One young man even fled naked as they had seized him by his clothing. How many people are willing to follow Jesus when it is dangerous to be his follower? There have been many martyrs throughout the history of the Christian faith, and there are many martyrs for the faith today. These courageous people are exceptional and are only a small fraction of those who call themselves Christians. Do we have the courage and the faithfulness to stand in the face of danger for the sake of Jesus Christ? Would we not be more likely to desert him if our lives or our security were threatened? Would we flee naked into the night?

<u>The Trial of Jesus before Annas and Caiaphas the High Priests</u>
In John 18:19-24 (NRSV), "Then the high priest questioned Jesus about his disciples and about his teaching. Jesus answered, 'I have

spoken openly to the world; I have always taught in synagogues and in the temple, where all the Jews come together. I have said nothing in secret. Why do you ask me? Ask those who heard what I said to them; they know what I said.' When he had said this, one of the police standing nearby struck Jesus on the face, saying, 'Is that how you answer the high priest?' Jesus answered, 'If I have spoken wrongly, testify to the wrong. But if I have spoken rightly, why do you strike me?' Then Annas sent him bound to Caiaphas the high priest."

Jesus was perceived as a threat to those who held power over the people of Israel. The Romans had conquered Israel and put the compliant people into positions of power and administration who would cooperate with the Romans in their exploitation of the people. The Romans were interested in keeping the peace so that they could maximize the wealth gained through taxes from the people of Israel. The Romans were conquerors who were relatively indifferent to the religion and culture of the people that they conquered, as long as there was no trouble and the heavy burden of taxes they imposed were paid. Those who served the Romans were hated by the people, but the traitors had the support and might of the Roman Empire behind them.

Israel was a theocracy, which was ruled by the temple priests in Jerusalem. In order to keep their positions of power, they had to keep any real or imagined threat to the status quo suppressed. Jesus was perceived as a threat to their power because of his popularity, the gospel that he preached, and his opposition to the corruption of the temple. Jesus was a Galilean and therefore was suspect since he was not a Judean. From the perspective of those who served Roman interests, Jesus appeared to be trouble and he would be eliminated before he became more of a threat to their power. Capital punishment was common in those days for a multitude of crimes and his guilt was a foregone conclusion before he was even arrested. It was only a question of who would take responsibility for his summary execution, and who had the authority to execute him. Jesus understood this and simply pointed out the hypocrisy of his trial. Jesus was murdered by the Roman occupying army, eliminated as a potential threat to Roman order, and complicit with the Roman controlled theocracy of Judea.

Jesus before Herod

In Luke 23:6-12 (NRSV), "When Pilate heard this, he asked whether the man was a Galilean. And when he learned that he was under Herod's jurisdiction, he sent him off to Herod, who was himself in Jerusalem at that time. When Herod saw Jesus, he was very glad, for he had been wanting to see him for a long time, because he had heard about him and was hoping to see him perform some sign. He questioned him at some length, but Jesus gave him no answer. The chief priests and the scribes stood by, vehemently accusing him. Even Herod with his soldiers treated him with contempt and mocked him; then he put an elegant robe on him, and sent him back to Pilate. That same day Herod and Pilate became friends with each other; before this they had been enemies."

Jesus was shuffled around Jerusalem by the temple priests in an attempt to find someone who would execute him based on their false charges against him as a blasphemer and revolutionary. Herod was the ruler of Galilee and had been seeking the death of Jesus for several years. Miraculously, Jesus had eluded him during his ministry in Galilee. Herod the Great, father of Herod, had tried to kill Jesus at his birth in Bethlehem. This Herod, son of Herod the Great, had murdered John the Baptist and was anxious to eliminate Jesus. Herod was aware of Jesus' power and attempted to force Jesus into performing for him. Jesus would not perform for him, so he is therefore humiliated and sent to Pilate to be executed by the Romans. Jesus fully understood what he was doing and where it would lead. He was not going to entertain Herod for the amusement of the court.

The Trial before Pilate

In John 18:28-40 (NRSV), "Then they took Jesus from Caiaphas to Pilate's headquarters. It was early in the morning. They themselves did not enter the headquarters, so as to avoid ritual defilement and to be able to eat the Passover. So Pilate went out to them and said, 'What accusation do you bring against this man?' They answered, 'If this man were not a criminal, we would not have handed him over to you.' Pilate said to them, 'Take him yourselves and judge him according to your law.' The Jews replied, 'We are not permitted to put anyone to death.' (This was to fulfill what Jesus had said when he indicated the kind of death he was to die.) Then Pilate entered the headquarters again, summoned Jesus, and asked him, 'Are you the King of the Jews?' Jesus answered, 'Do you ask this on your own, or did others tell you about me?' Pilate replied, 'I am not a Jew, am I? Your own nation and the chief priests have handed you over to me. What have you done?' Jesus answered, 'My kingdom is not from this world. If my kingdom were from this world, my followers would be fighting to keep me from being handed over to the Jews. But as it is, my kingdom is not from here.' Pilate asked him, 'So you are a king?' Jesus answered, 'You say that I am a king. For this I was born, and for this I came into the world, to testify to the truth. Everyone who belongs to the truth listens to my voice.' Pilate asked him, 'What is truth?' After he had said this, he went out to the Jews again and told them, 'I find no case against him. But you have a custom that I release someone for you at the Passover. Do you want me to release for you the King of the Jews?' They shouted in reply, 'Not this man, but Barabbas!' Now Barabbas was a bandit."

The governor of Judea, Pontius Pilate, found no basis for the execution of Jesus. He would have been indifferent to the fate of Jesus, except the crowds representing the temple officials were insistent on the death of Jesus. Ironically, Pilate gave them the choice between a proven revolutionary and Jesus who was not a political revolutionary. Evidently, Jesus was perceived as more of a threat to them than the rebel Barabbas. Without knowing it, they were correct, since governments come and go, but the gospel of Jesus Christ is forever. The gospel of Jesus Christ has influenced the world far more than any political system. Beyond their understanding, they had chosen the ultimate sacrifice for human sin in the death of Jesus Christ. "What is truth?" Pilate asks. To some, truth is relative and can be confabulated. To people of faith, there are absolute truths.

The Suffering of Jesus
In John 19:1-16 (NRSV), "Then Pilate took Jesus and had him flogged. And the soldiers wove a crown of thorns and put it on his head, and they dressed him in a purple robe. They kept coming up to him, saying, 'Hail, King of the Jews!' and striking him on the face. Pilate went out again and said to them, 'Look, I am bringing him out to you to let you know that I find no case against him.' So Jesus came out, wearing the crown of thorns and the purple robe. Pilate said to them, 'Here is the man!' When the chief priests and the police saw him, they shouted, 'Crucify him! Crucify him!' Pilate said to them, 'Take him yourselves and crucify him; I find no case against him.' The Jews answered him, 'We have a law, and according to that law he ought to die because he has claimed to be the Son of God.' Now when Pilate heard this, he was more afraid than ever. He entered his headquarters again and asked Jesus, 'Where are you from?' But Jesus gave him no answer. Pilate therefore said to him, 'Do you refuse to speak to me? Do you not know that I have power to release you, and power to crucify you?' Jesus answered him, 'You would have no power over me unless it had been given you from above; therefore the one who handed me over to you is guilty of a greater sin.' From then on Pilate tried to release him, but the Jews cried out, 'If you release this man, you are no friend of the emperor. Everyone who claims to be a king sets himself against the emperor.' When Pilate heard these words, he brought Jesus outside and sat on the judge's bench at a place

called The Stone Pavement, or in Hebrew Gabbatha. Now it was the day of Preparation for the Passover; and it was about noon. He said to the Jews, 'Here is your King!' They cried out, 'Away with him! Away with him! Crucify him!' Pilate asked them, 'Shall I crucify your King?' The chief priests answered, 'We have no king but the emperor.' Then he handed him over to them to be crucified."

Pilate thought he could appease the crowd that sought the death of Jesus by having him severely flogged. Flogging was often fatal because the whip that was used contained small sharp pieces of bone and glass that were tied into the ends of the whip, so that the back of the victim was flayed. Jesus survived the flogging and Pilate presented him half dead to the temple crowd. They wanted his complete humiliation and destruction. Crucifixion was the cruelest and most demeaning death known in the Roman Empire, reserved for only the worst criminals. Jesus not only died for us, but he suffered emotionally and physically the worst torment the world could devise at that time. He took upon himself all the sins of the world. He took your sins and mine upon himself. He chose to do this for you. By his wounds we have been healed. When we suffer, we are reminded of Jesus' terrible suffering for us.

The Road to the Cross
In Luke 23:26-31 (NRSV), "As they led him away, they seized a man, Simon of Cyrene, who was coming from the country, and they laid the cross on him, and made him carry it behind Jesus. A great number of the people followed him, and among them were women who were beating their breasts and wailing for him. But Jesus turned to them and said, 'Daughters of Jerusalem, do not weep for me, but weep for yourselves and for your children. For the days are surely coming when they will say, "Blessed are the barren, and the wombs that never bore, and the breasts that never nursed." Then they will begin to say to the mountains, "Fall on us"; and to the hills, "Cover us." For if they do this when the wood is green, what will happen when it is dry?'"

The disciples of Jesus fled for fear of their lives, and a few supporters who had the courage to witness the events of his trial and execution could only weep at the suffering of the Son of God. Because of his rejection by men, he knew that there was going to be more war and suffering in the world. Jesus had foretold the destruction of Jerusalem and the nation of Israel which would take place in three decades. When people choose power and war over the gospel of peace, they will suffer the consequences of their choice. Jesus is warning the women that the suffering of the world is going to be worse for them. How has the world changed in the past 2000 years? Are we any different than the people of Jerusalem? How many millions of innocent children and women have died in wars in the past centuries?

The Cross
In John 19:17-27 (NRSV), "And carrying the cross by himself, he went out to what is called The Place of the Skull, which in Hebrew is called Golgotha. There they crucified him, and with him two others, one on either side, with Jesus between them. Pilate also had an inscription written and put on the cross. It read, 'Jesus of Nazareth, the King of the Jews.' Many of the Jews read this inscription, because the place where Jesus was crucified was near the city; and it was written in Hebrew, in Latin, and in Greek. Then the chief priests of the Jews said to Pilate, 'Do not write, "The King of the Jews," but, "This man said, I am King of the Jews."' Pilate answered, 'What I have written I have written.' When the soldiers had crucified Jesus, they took his clothes and divided them into four parts, one for each soldier. They also took his tunic; now the tunic was seamless, woven in one piece from the top. So they said to one another, 'Let us not tear it, but cast lots for it to see who will get it.' This was to fulfill what the scripture says, 'They divided my clothes among themselves, and for my clothing they cast lots.' And that is what the soldiers did. Meanwhile, standing near the cross of Jesus were his mother, and his mother's sister, Mary the wife of

Clopas, and Mary Magdalene. When Jesus saw his mother and the disciple whom he loved standing beside her, he said to his mother, 'Woman, here is your son.' Then he said to the disciple, 'Here is your mother.' And from that hour the disciple took her into his own home."

The official charge against Jesus was nailed to the cross, which read that he had claimed he was King of the Jews. This was both true and untrue. Jesus had indeed claimed that he was the Messiah and, according to some people's understanding of the Messiah, that would mean being a king of the Jewish people. For some people, the messianic expectation was on a conquering king who would rule the world, setting the people of Israel up as the dominant nation while all other nations would serve her. This was not the understanding of the Messiah that Jesus had. He described himself as the suffering servant whom the prophet Isaiah had envisioned as the Messiah. Jesus had no interest in political, military, or economic power. Jesus was a king and is a king, but not of this world. Even his disciples did not fully understand us this. Do we as disciples of Jesus Christ fully appreciate his kingship? Jesus is King because he would reign in the hearts and minds of all people.

Jesus was completely abandoned by his followers, except for women and one young disciple. Even in his agony on the cross, his compassion for others caused him to speak to the young disciple to care for his mother. Jesus was the embodiment of the love of God and this is evident even in his dying on the cross.

Jesus Mocked on the Cross

In Matthew 27:39-48 (NRSV), "Those who passed by derided him, shaking their heads and saying, 'You who would destroy the temple and build it in three days, save yourself! If you are the Son of God, come down from the cross.' In the same way the chief priests also, along with the scribes and elders, were mocking him, saying, 'He saved others; he cannot save himself. He is the King of Israel;

let him come down from the cross now, and we will believe in him. He trusts in God; let God deliver him now, if he wants to; for he said, "I am God's Son."' The bandits who were crucified with him also taunted him in the same way. From noon on, darkness came over the whole land until three in the afternoon. And about three o'clock Jesus cried with a loud voice, 'Eli, Eli, lema sabachthani?' that is, 'My God, my God, why have you forsaken me?' When some of the bystanders heard it, they said, 'This man is calling for Elijah.' At once one of them ran and got a sponge, filled it with sour wine, put it on a stick, and gave it to him to drink."

Jesus could have rescued himself from the cross if he had wanted to. But he chose to stay nailed to that cruel wood because he was obedient to the higher purpose of God in defeating the power of death, by his death and resurrection. The people who mocked him seem so despicable, but would it be any different today? People who try to follow the example of Jesus in today's world are often mocked and despised. Even a saintly person like Mother Theresa had detractors who wrote books trying to destroy her reputation.

On the cross, Jesus suffered the absolute depths of despair. When he cried out, he was quoting the first verse of Psalm 22 (NRSV): "My God, my God, why have you forsaken me?" This psalm describes precisely the suffering that he was going through, and it describes his triumph over suffering and death. When we read this psalm, we can have a sense of the extent of Jesus' torment. Even though he was the Son of God, in his agony he experienced being abandoned by God, but his faith in God was stronger than his feelings. The psalm concludes with the praise of God and triumph of God, as does the life of Jesus. Is our faith in God stronger than our feelings?

The Two Thieves
In Luke 23:39-47 (NRSV), "One of the criminals who were hanged there kept deriding him and saying, 'Are you not the Messiah? Save yourself and us!' But the other rebuked him, saying, 'Do you not

fear God, since you are under the same sentence of condemnation? And we indeed have been condemned justly, for we are getting what we deserve for our deeds, but this man has done nothing wrong.' Then he said, 'Jesus, remember me when you come into your kingdom.' He replied, 'Truly I tell you, today you will be with me in Paradise.' It was now about noon, and darkness came over the whole land until three in the afternoon, while the sun's light failed; and the curtain of the temple was torn in two. Then Jesus, crying with a loud voice, said, 'Father, into your hands I commend my spirit.' Having said this, he breathed his last. When the centurion saw what had taken place, he praised God and said, 'Certainly this man was innocent.'"

There were two thieves on crosses on either side of Jesus; one of them mocked Jesus and the other put his faith in Jesus. Even while he was dying on the cross, this convicted criminal confessed his guilt and believed in Jesus Christ. Jesus told this man that he would be with him and taken up into paradise this day. And so shall anyone who has faith in Jesus Christ be taken up into heaven the day they die in this world. This is the choice that we are confronted with in our lives.

The day Jesus was murdered was the worst and the best day in the history of the world. We killed the Son of God. He won our eternal salvation on the cross. The world was cast into darkness, but the full love of God was revealed for the first time to humankind. This was the day of the most extreme contrast of dark and light, good and evil in the history of the world. What is good about Good Friday? This was the day of salvation for the world.

The Death of Jesus
In John 19:28-35 (NRSV), "After this, when Jesus knew that all was now finished, he said (in order to fulfill the scripture), 'I am thirsty.' A jar full of sour wine was standing there. So they put a sponge full of the wine on a branch of hyssop and held it to his

mouth. When Jesus had received the wine, he said, 'It is finished.' Then he bowed his head and gave up his spirit. Since it was the day of Preparation, the Jews did not want the bodies left on the cross during the Sabbath, especially because that Sabbath was a day of great solemnity. So they asked Pilate to have the legs of the crucified men broken and the bodies removed. Then the soldiers came and broke the legs of the first and of the other who had been crucified with him. But when they came to Jesus and saw that he was already dead, they did not break his legs. Instead, one of the soldiers pierced his side with a spear, and at once blood and water came out. (He who saw this has testified so that you also may believe. His testimony is true, and he knows that he tells the truth.)."

Jesus experienced mortality in his death on the cross. How can we comprehend a love so great that he would lay aside his divinity and take upon himself our mortality? He even took upon himself the shame and horror of death on a cross. To ensure that he was truly dead, he was stabbed in the side with a spear, and blood and fluid poured out of the wound. Medically, this is exactly what would happen if the dead person were stabbed. This assured the Roman soldiers that he was indeed dead.

Jesus died for us, so that we might have eternal life. We are all going to die, and by our faith in Jesus we may have eternal life with him in Heaven. This is the gift of God that we have been given if we choose it. This is the gift of God that we have to proclaim to our brothers and sisters.

CHAPTER 6

HIS LOVE

Jesus is all about love. In John 13:34 (NRSV), he says, "I give you a new commandment, that you love one another. Just as I have loved you, you also should love one another." We are not to define love any way we fancy; rather, we are to love as he loved. This is a really big distinction between how our culture defines love and how Jesus loved. Growing up, my generation was greatly influenced by popular music of the day. The music industry catered to the frenzy of sexual impulses in the teenage population that bought the records. Love was the major theme of most of the music. Intentionally, the understanding of love in the rock and roll was sexual. Our hormones were out of control and the lyrics of sexual innuendo were easily understood. The emphasis on the strong beat aroused our passions. Dancing was foreplay. We equated love completely with sex. This is not at all what Jesus was referring to in his numerous teachings on the importance of love. Sexuality is a separate issue from love. What did Jesus want us to know about God's love?

<u>God's Love</u>
The love of God cannot be adequately described in words because human language is incapable of expressing the perfect

nature of God. We strive to communicate the love that we have experienced from Jesus, but it is so frustrating because his love goes far beyond our ability to put it into words. The Bible tells us "God is love," and all love comes from God. What we know as love is only a small fraction of the fullness of God's love. Our human understanding of God's love is like a few drops of water compared to the oceans of the world. To know the love of Christ is to become aware of the oceans of love that lie before us. Jesus gives numerous specific examples and teaching on what God's love is and what it looks like.

God's love is awesome to behold. Too often, people are afraid to accept his love because they do not trust love from their experiences with people. We may be fearful that we will be rejected since we have been rejected by people so many times in the past. We may be afraid that we are not good enough since we have been told we are not good enough so many times in our lives. How many people have been told they are terrible sinners by the church? Would God reject us just as we have been rejected? Our shame and anger causes us to turn our back on God's love. We may be reluctant to risk giving up control of our lives; we like to think that we have been in control of our lives. What would happen to us if God asked us to do something that we did not want to do? How are we to survive and keep what we have worked so hard to acquire if God asked us to make sacrifices? What would happen to our sinful pleasures if we had to give them up? What will become of our ego if we submit ourselves to God? If we allow the love of God to invade our heart, we will become vulnerable, and the concepts that have ruled our lives will be at risk. Is the love of Christ worth taking a chance on, when we may lose something? Can we trust loving God?

The love of Christ will never make us do anything we do not want to do. Love is patient and kind so that we will grow in our love of Christ according to our willingness and ability. As we take little baby steps towards God, God takes giant steps towards us. The blessings that we receive by far exceed our slow and unsteady progress towards God. We are constantly rewarded with the incentive of more love. God is not withholding the love from us; rather, in our growth and acceptance of the Spirit of Christ, we are increasing in our ability to accept the love of God.

To a baby Christian, the life of a mature Christian may seem very scary, because they have willingly sacrificed so much of the things that we are unwilling to let go of at this stage in our discipleship. St. Paul was the epitome of a wise and mature Christian. After decades into his discipleship, giving himself over freely to the Spirit of Christ, in Philippians 3:7-9 (NRSV), he wrote, "Yet whatever gains I had, these I have come to regard as loss because of Christ. More than that, I regard everything as loss because of the surpassing value of knowing Christ Jesus my Lord. For his sake I have suffered the loss of all things, and I regard them as rubbish, in order that I may gain Christ and be found in him, not having a righteousness of my own that comes from the law, but one that comes through faith in Christ, the righteousness from God based on faith." May we ever arrive at the level of maturity that St. Paul was? Only if we want to, and only by the grace of God will we become as wise and full of the Spirit of Christ like St. Paul. Those people who are so full of the Spirit of Christ have been called the saints. May we strive to be like them.

The love of God is unconditional love. This love is given with no strings attached. When we receive this love, we are compelled to respond to it by becoming more loving ourselves and transforming our lives to the nature of Christ. Jesus said in John 15:13 (NRSV), "No one has greater love than this, to lay down one's life for one's friends." This love of God is to put the interests of others ahead of our own. This is contrary to human nature but it is absolutely the nature of God's love. In Greek this is called agape love. Agape love is different than brotherly love or erotic love. Agape is the love of Jesus Christ. He lived this love, and asks us to follow him.

Jesus' Love

Jesus was willing to sacrifice his life for us. His sacrifice was not only in his death, but his sacrifice was also coming into this world. He gave up his divinity and took on the form of a humble servant to all people. He submitted himself to all the temptations that we experience and he suffered all the pain that we feel. He was tempted, but he never gave in to the temptations. The difference between us and Jesus is that he never sinned and we are all too familiar with sin.

In the scorching of the lash, he was whipped almost to the point of death. We read in the prophet Isaiah 53:5 (NRSV), "by his bruises we are healed." He told his disciples that love of God could lead them to the ultimate sacrifice. In the Christian tradition, we are informed that they all died a martyr's death. We are reminded once again, Jesus said, "No one has greater love than this, to lay down one's life for one's friends," John 15:13 (NRSV). The little sacrifices that we make are insignificant compared to the lives of the martyrs. His love was to take the consequences of our sin upon himself so that we would be acceptable to God.

Jesus was the ultimate sacrifice of God's self. In John 3:16-17 (NRSV), we read, "For God so loved the world that he gave his only Son, so that everyone who believes in him may not perish but may have eternal life. Indeed, God did not send the Son into the world to condemn the world, but in order that the world might be saved through him." The Son of God is the love of God, and the creative activity of God in the world. What Jesus experienced was God's experience. What Jesus thought and felt was also God's experience. God in Jesus was not merely a divine linkage; they are one. The love of God demands a response. Shall we open our hearts to this tremendous outpouring of love?

Our Love

Everybody is looking for love. We want to give love and we want to be loved. Too often, we seek love in inappropriate ways because we do not know how to give or receive love. We were put in this world to love God, and to love our neighbor as ourselves. This is the purpose of our life and there is no other purpose. The Holy Bible is crystal clear on this matter.

In 1 John 4:7-10 (NRSV), "Beloved, let us love one another, because love is from God; everyone who loves is born of God and knows God. Whoever does not love does not know God, for God is love. God's love was revealed among us in this way: God sent his only Son into the world so that we might live through him. In this is love, not that we loved God but that he loved us and sent his Son to be the atoning sacrifice for our sins." God has demonstrated to us in Jesus a love beyond our comprehension, and by his forgiveness of our sins makes it possible for us to share in the ultimate love, which is the love of God. The indwelling Spirit of Christ will teach us how to love, and help us receive love of God. To know God is to share the love of Christ with our brothers and sisters. This is what we were created to do. This love is who we were created to be.

Perhaps the hardest thing in the world to do is to express love appropriately. On a superficial level, it seems like the simplest thing to express love, but humans are extremely complex and unpredictable beings, which makes meaningful relationships extremely difficult. Much of the time, we do not know how to love appropriately, so we must rely on the guidance of the Holy Spirit to teach us how to love. We can also learn from the teachings of Jesus; for example, in John 14:23-24 (NRSV), "Jesus answered him, 'Those who love me will keep my word, and my Father will love them, and we will come to them and make our home with them. Whoever does not love me does not keep my words; and the word that you hear is not mine, but is from the Father who sent me.'" We have the promise of God that by the presence of the Holy Spirit we will learn how to love and to receive love. It is a process that takes a lifetime and more. This is the ultimate learning experience because this is the curriculum of life.

A follower of Jesus Christ walks in the way of Christ. You shall know them by their fruits. The follower of Jesus Christ would never promote prejudice, fear, or hatred of another human being. Jesus taught us that we should love our enemies. He taught us that we should stand for the truth and resist evil. We have the right to defend ourselves against evil, but we do this out of our love for God and our love for our brothers and sisters. Jesus told his disciples in John 15:9-13 (NRSV), "As the Father has loved me, so I have loved you; abide in my love. If you keep my commandments, you will abide in my love, just as I have kept my Father's commandments and abide in his love. I have said these things to you so that my joy may be in you, and that your joy may be complete. This is my commandment, that you love one another as I have loved you. No one has greater love than this, to lay down one's life for one's friends." This is not optional, for this is the primary commandment to every person who claims to be a Christian.

The Whole Creation Proclaims God is Love

This world and all the creatures in it were made as an expression of God's love. We were made by love to be an expression of God's love. The single most important act of love in human history was the life, death, and resurrection of Jesus. All of life is a gift from God; it is all grace. The ultimate experience of grace is to know the living person of the chosen one of God, Jesus Christ. By knowing him, we receive grace upon grace.

In Ephesians 2:4-8 (NRSV), "But God, who is rich in mercy, out of the great love with which he loved us even when we were dead through our trespasses, made us alive together with Christ— by grace you have been saved— and raised us up with him and seated us with him in the heavenly places in Christ Jesus, so that in the ages to come he might show the immeasurable riches of his grace in kindness toward us in Christ Jesus. For by grace you have been saved through faith, and this is not your own doing; it is the gift of God." How we receive and share this grace has eternal consequences. Our choices in this world will determine where we go in the life after this world. Why do people work and study so thoroughly about making a purchase, and pay so little attention to the state of their soul? Everything in this world will perish sooner or later, but the soul lives after this existence on this little planet. We have been given a gift we have neither earned nor deserved. What possible reason do we have for rejecting this gift of salvation by faith in Jesus?

A Promise of Love
The most amazing statement of unending love was made by Jesus to his followers in John 14:1-4 (NRSV): "Do not let your hearts be troubled. Believe in God, believe also in me. In my Father's house there are many dwelling places. If it were not so, would I have told you that I go to prepare a place for you? And if I go and prepare a place for you, I will come again and will take you to myself, so that where I am, there you may be also. And you know the way to the place where I am going." This love promises us a place in heaven. Jesus will come to us when we die and take us to heaven. There is nothing comparable in any other religion. How could a person reject this offer? To reject this is to reject heaven. This is the love of God in his promise to us. Love is drawn to Love. That is the mystery of life.

CHAPTER 7
HIS FORGIVENESS

"Father, forgive them; for they do not know what they are doing," Jesus said from the cross, looking down over the people who had crucified him in Luke 23:34 (NRSV). Jesus came into this world to live with us, to teach us, to love, to heal us, to save us, and to show us the way to eternal life. For this, he was beaten, mocked, whipped, spat upon, and crucified. The people that did this to him were his people, and he loved them in spite of what they did to him. We are also his people. What they did to him, is what we do to him. This is called the atonement. He loves us, even though we continue to mock him and crucify him. He looks upon us, forgives us, and loves us because he created us. His desire is that we follow his commandments and come home to heaven.

We have been forgiven for two thousand years, but his forgiveness is not completed until we receive it. His forgiveness is offered to us freely. He only asks us that we accept his forgiveness. Forgiveness is not a one-way street. It has to be received. Do we believe in his forgiveness? Do we receive his forgiveness? Do we live as forgiven people? Do we forgive as we have been forgiven? Why has Jesus forgiven us since we are all guilty of sins of thought, word, and deed?

Forgiveness is an act of healing. The broken is made whole. The injured is repaired. The world is often a difficult and painful experience in which everyone suffers. There is more hurt in the world than we know. Everyone is wounded. Everyone is broken. Everyone needs healing. Without reconciliation (which is the purpose of forgiveness) the wounds increase. This is the power of sin and death. We have the opportunity to heal our relationships by seeking and giving forgiveness. We forgive because we have been forgiven.

To forgive someone of an injustice that they have done to us is an act of reconciliation. The purpose of reconciliation is to break down the barrier that exists between two people when an intentional wrong has been done by one of the parties. It is difficult for a person to forgive because it goes against human nature. Our baser instincts are to seek revenge against the person who has hurt us. We want to express our anger. We want to strike back. We want revenge! We want them to suffer for what they have done to us. Forgiveness goes against our instinct to fight or flight. Human history is often taught as an ongoing series of wars and conflicts. The desire to dominate and exploit one another has led us to war after bloody war. Where has the power of forgiveness been in our long history? Forgiveness brings people together and conflicts tears us apart. Why is it so difficult for us to forgive? Only when we know how much we have been forgiven can we begin to forgive others.

To forgive is to humble ourself. The forgiver and the forgiven have to put their pride aside, they have to put their anger aside, and they have to respect each other. The desire to be in relationship with another person has to be stronger than the desire to prove that we are right and they are wrong. It is easier to be complacent with our sense of rightness than it is to do the painful work of reconciliation. Why do we always have to be right? We need the love of God to give us the desire to work for reconciliation and find forgiveness in our hearts. We pray for forgiveness and to be forgiving people. Jesus taught us to pray, "And forgive us our debts, as we also have forgiven our debtors," in Matthew 6:12 (NRSV). Only God can give us forgiveness for all the separation we have created between ourselves and God. Only the Holy Spirit can equip us to truly forgive.

How could it be possible that Jesus would forgive us? It is only possible because he was both fully human and fully divine. If he had been only human, he could never have said, "Father, forgive them; for they do not know what they are doing," Luke 23:34 (NRSV). This is not what an innocent man says as he is being tortured to death, hanging on a cross. It is an act of faith to believe in his divine forgiveness. If he truly forgives us our sins, then he must have been divine. Because he was divine, then he was capable of forgiving us our sins. If he was not divine, he was delusional to forgive us, and it means nothing. Since he truly was divine our sins have been forgiven. "But so that you may know that the Son of Man has authority on earth to forgive sins," Mark 2:10 (NRSV). When you believe that Jesus was the divine revelation of God, then you know that you have been forgiven and only have to trust in him.

We say that we believe in him, and that we believe that he has forgiven us our sins. Do we? Do we really believe that we have been forgiven? If we are honest with ourselves, we know that we are sinners. We may know intellectually that Jesus has forgiven our sins. Without emotionally experiencing forgiveness, there is something missing; this is how humans function. We must really feel Jesus loves us. That is why he has forgiven you. To know this, you must receive him into your heart. When and only when you know him intimately can you understand and accept his forgiveness. When you have asked him into your heart, you will know his great love for you. He knows everything that you have ever done, he knows everything that you have ever thought, he knows your feelings, and he knows the consequences of your actions. Knowing you better than you know yourself, he loves you. He loves you far more than you are capable of understanding. There is no experience in this world that can prepare you for his love. He wants us to know him and to know his love. Our sin is the barrier that separates us from him, and he wants to dissolve that barrier. His forgiveness is his radical plan to reconcile you to himself and God. His forgiving us is the bridge that makes us able to reach him. The cross of Christ is the way God bridges the chasm that is between sinful humans and God. When you know him and his forgiveness in your life, it is never the same. It is as if our great burden has been lifted from us and we can begin to live free of the slavery to sin and death.

Living as a forgiven person is very different than living under the bondage to sin. Sin limits our choices. Freedom from the power of sin and death expands our choices. Freedom is having choices and not being a slave to sin. When we know God's forgiveness, we seek reconciliation with all people whenever possible. Even though we are aware of our baser instincts, they do not control us, because our chief desire is to do God's will. God's will is distinctly different than what is predictable human behavior. God's will is described as follows in the Gospel of Luke: "Be merciful, just as your Father is merciful. Do not judge, and you will not be judged; do not condemn, and you will not be condemned. Forgive, and you will be forgiven; give, and it will be given to you. A good measure, pressed down, shaken together, running over, will be put into your lap; for the measure you give will be the measure you get back," Luke 6:36-38 (NRSV). As we forgive, so shall we be forgiven. Our forgiveness was won by Jesus, and he asked us to forgive one another as he has forgiven us. This is real freedom.

Do we forgive as we have been forgiven? Jesus told the parable of "The Prodigal Son" in Luke 15:11-32. The younger son demanded his inheritance from his father and squandered his inheritance in debauchery. He returned to his father begging forgiveness. The father forgives him immediately and called for a great celebration. The elder son resented what his father had done for his brother and complained about it to his father. Most of us can relate to having been the prodigal son at some time in our life. Many of us can relate to being the elder son at certain times in our life. Jesus asks us to be like the father, being ready to give our forgiveness. This parable is the perfect lesson in forgiveness. If you read this parable many times and study it, you will understand the meaning of forgiveness.

We are invited into the reign of God by letting the Spirit of God rule our hearts. "For if you forgive others their trespasses, your heavenly Father will also forgive you; but if you do not forgive others, neither will your Father forgive your trespasses," Matthew 6:14-15 (NRSV). We must strive to be forgiving people. It is only through the power of the Holy Spirit that we can truly forgive. We need to ask God for the gift of forgiveness. Jesus was asked how many times we should forgive, and he told his disciples to forgive without limit in Matthew 18:21-22.

Why has Jesus forgiven us if we are all guilty of sin? The prophet Jeremiah, five hundred years before Jesus, was inspired by God to foretell of a new covenant God was to make with humans. In Jeremiah 31:31-35 (NRSV), "The days are surely coming, says the Lord, when I will make a new covenant with the house of Israel and the house of Judah. It will not be like the covenant that I made with their ancestors when I took them by the hand to bring them out of the land of Egypt—a covenant that they broke, though I was their husband, says the Lord. But this is the covenant that I will make with the house of Israel after those days, says the Lord: I will put my law within them, and I will write it on their hearts; and I will be their God, and they shall be my people. No longer shall they teach one another, or say to each other, 'Know the Lord,' for they shall all know me, from the least of them to the greatest, says the Lord; for I will forgive their iniquity, and remember their sin no more. Thus says the Lord, who gives the sun for light by day and the fixed order of the moon and the stars for light by night, who stirs up the sea so that its waves roar—the Lord of hosts is his name." This was a promise of God that was fulfilled by Jesus. This is the New Covenant. Through his sacrifice, the perfect and final sacrifice was made for the forgiveness of sin. In the letter to the Hebrews, this is explained in detail. Jesus was God's fulfillment of many promises and we are the beneficiaries of God's plan of salvation.

It is the plan of God that people will be reconciled to God and all those who want to be saved can be saved through the salvation of Jesus Christ. Jesus Christ is the New Covenant between God and humankind. We have the opportunity to be a participant in this new world, this new covenant with God, or we can be opposed to it. Indifference is the same as opposition. God does not coerce us. God invites us. We are given this choice freely and this determines our eternal destiny. The consequences of our decision will have consequences for the entire human future. The ripples of our lives impact other lives in ways we have no knowledge of in this world. We are not isolated events; rather, we are all connected in mysterious ways. Our faith is not exclusively about our own salvation. Our faith is about the salvation of the whole world. We cannot comprehend the magnitude of God's plan, but we live by faith in God's plan for the salvation of the world.

To refuse the gift of forgiveness is to reject God. This is a grievous sin and needs to be taken seriously. Carrying guilt after we have asked for forgiveness is a rejection of the gift. Faith in Jesus is letting go of guilt once we have sincerely asked for forgiveness. There is no limit to forgiveness. Jesus wants us to live in peace with God and our sisters and brothers. It is essential we let God be our God. As we forgive so shall we be forgiven.

CHAPTER 8
WOMEN AND JESUS

The interactions between Jesus and women are vitally important, because women have been oppressed for thousands of years and are still oppressed today. What does the Gospel record show us about Jesus' relationships with women? Jesus is the supreme example for our behavior. Our cultural background shapes us, but we can look critically at our assumptions and attitudes and evaluate them in comparison with Jesus. It is amazing so many of the events of Jesus in relation with women have survived, since the prevailing thought of the Greco-Roman world of the early church was vigorously misogynistic. It is not an exaggeration to state the ancient world valued women as sex objects and mothers, and gave women no status in society. Women were completely exploited and abused in the ancient world. The Biblical examples demonstrate how Jesus interacted with women, completely unlike the prevailing cultural norm.

<u>Mary the Mother of Jesus</u>
The most important woman in Jesus' life was his mother, Mary. We know very little about the details of the relationship between Jesus and his Mother. In Luke 2:40 (NRSV), we learn, "The child

grew and became strong, filled with wisdom; and the favor of God was upon him." This statement reveals much about Jesus and his mother. Because Jesus was fully human, he grew from ignorance to wisdom during his childhood. His divine nature became part of his developing awareness as he matured.

This statement informs us that Mary was an exceptional mother. It is safe to assume Mary cultivated his character, his education, and his relation with God. At some unknown point, Jesus' father died and Mary was a single parent who raised Jesus. Because Mary knew through divine revelation the divinity of Jesus, she was aware of the extraordinary task before her of raising the Messiah. What a responsibility for a young mother with no formal education, and living a subsistence existence under oppressive Roman occupation. Mary had other children to raise as well, and life would have been a daily struggle for survival to feed, clothe, and shelter her family. "The child grew and became strong, filled with wisdom; and the favor of God was upon him," Luke 2:40 (NRSV). This principal experience of Mary shaped all of his subsequent relations with women. Jesus treated women respectfully. He engaged women with the same dignity with which he engaged men. Jesus did not observe the prejudices of his male companions or their cultural bias. After Jesus' death, the early church backed away from Jesus' radical appreciation of women, and put women in a secondary role in the church. The dominance of the Greco–Roman world compromised the radical feminism of Jesus. The full participation of women in the church is only recently emerging in some parts of the church universal.

There is an interesting event in the Gospel of John 2:1-11 where Jesus is ordered by his mother to perform the miracle of turning water into wine, at the wedding in Cana. There is a delightful exchange between Mary and Jesus where Mary orders Jesus to change the water into wine against his initial response to not do this. This is the very beginning of his ministry, and is his first miracle. As a result of this miracle, "his disciples believed in him,"

John 2:11 (NRSV). Mary was empowering him to be the Messiah. Mother Mary knew best.

At the crucifixion, Mary was present at the foot of the cross with the disciple John. In Jesus' dying breath and acute pain, his concern was for the care of his beloved Mother. "Meanwhile, standing near the cross of Jesus were his mother, and his mother's sister, Mary the wife of Clopas, and Mary Magdalene. When Jesus saw his mother and the disciple whom he loved standing beside her, he said to his mother, 'Woman, here is your son.' Then he said to the disciple, 'Here is your mother.' And from that hour the disciple took her into his own home," John 19:25-27 (NRSV). Putting Mary in the care of John ensured she would be protected and cared for as long as she lived. There is a reliable tradition in Ephesus, Turkey, that John took Mary there and cared for her for the rest of her life, away from the persecutions in the Holy Land. On the cross, the incarnation of God's concern was for his mother. This speaks volumes for his love for her. How Mary must have suffered witnessing the crucifixion, and looking up at her son dying in agony, thinking of her. Jesus showed this compassion for women in many other instances in his life.

The Woman Caught in Adultery

Jesus often confronted the oppression of women directly at his own peril. One of the most striking examples is when he confronts an angry mob which is about to stone a woman to death. Keep in mind that men in the Greco-Roman world were never punished for adultery, only women. The punishment for women was death by stoning. It is significant that this injustice of stoning women is still practiced today in parts of the world. The stoning of women for adultery is plainly designed to keep women in their place as subservient to men. Men are free to be predators of women, but a woman is a slave to her husband. This is the injustice Jesus confronted. Jesus was a radical supporter of women's rights, two thousand years ago.

In John 8:3-11 (NRSV), "The scribes and the Pharisees brought a woman who had been caught in adultery; and making her stand before all of them, they said to him, 'Teacher, this woman was caught in the very act of committing adultery. Now in the law Moses commanded us to stone such women. Now what do you say?' They said this to test him, so that they might have some charge to bring against him. Jesus bent down and wrote with his finger on the ground. When they kept on questioning him, he straightened up and said to them, 'Let anyone among you who is without sin be the first to throw a stone at her.' And once again he bent down and wrote on the ground. When they heard it, they went away, one by one, beginning with the elders; and Jesus was left alone with the woman standing before him. Jesus straightened up and said to her, 'Woman, where are they? Has no one condemned you?' She said, 'No one, sir.' And Jesus said, 'Neither do I condemn you. Go your way, and from now on do not sin again.'"

Jesus forced the accusers and executioners of this woman to deal with their own sinfulness. How many of them had used the services of prostitutes? How many of them had attempted to seduce women? How were they adulterous in thought, word, and deed? Jesus demanded they examine their own sins and, when they did, they turned and walked away. After Jesus and the woman were left alone, he forgave her and told her to sin no more. Jesus both saved her from death and freed her from her sins. A major doctrine in Christianity is that Jesus saves us from the power of sin and death. In this instance, Jesus did precisely that work of salvation for this woman. We might seriously see this example as how Jesus frees us from the power of sin and death.

<u>Jesus Teaches Mary</u>
Jesus was an itinerant rabbi who had many disciples and students. In his day, women were not allowed to be disciples or students of rabbis, but Jesus had women disciples and students. Mary, sister of Lazarus, was one of his students who is described learning from

him. This event is described in Luke 10:38-42. Students sat at the feet of the teacher. This was not a place for women. The male disciples may have been shocked by this breach of custom, or they may have gotten used to Jesus accepting women as students by this time. Mary's sister was not going to tolerate her sister taking the role of student while she busied herself with the traditional work of hospitality for the guests. "She had a sister named Mary, who sat at the Lord's feet and listened to what he was saying," Luke 10:39 (NRSV). This episode is about more than sibling rivalry. It is about women learning from Jesus just as men did. The jealousy of Martha, her sister, is explicit in the dialogue. Too often, women have been obstructions to the advancement of women. Two thousand years ago, a woman complained about a sister who wanted to learn from Jesus. Jesus rebuked Martha for criticizing Mary.

It has only been possible in recent times for some women in the world to receive education equal to men. Just a few generations ago, women were not admitted to schools of higher learning. Today, young women are murdered for attending school in parts of the world. What possible purpose does denying education to women serve except to keep them oppressed? Jesus confronted this injustice directly. A follower of Jesus would support the education of women without hesitation. Women are just as important to Jesus as men. Jesus demanded legal justice and equal education for women in a world where this was unthinkable.

The Canaanite Woman
One of the most intriguing interactions with a woman occurs outside of Israel. In Matthew 15:21-28 (NRSV), "Jesus left that place and went away to the district of Tyre and Sidon. Just then a Canaanite woman from that region came out and started shouting, 'Have mercy on me, Lord, Son of David; my daughter is tormented by a demon.' But he did not answer her at all. And his disciples came and urged him, saying, 'Send her away, for she keeps shouting after us.' He answered, 'I was sent only to the lost sheep of the

house of Israel.' But she came and knelt before him, saying, 'Lord, help me.' He answered, 'It is not fair to take the children's food and throw it to the dogs.' She said, 'Yes, Lord, yet even the dogs eat the crumbs that fall from their masters' table.' Then Jesus answered her, 'Woman, great is your faith! Let it be done for you as you wish.' And her daughter was healed instantly.'"

This exchange has to be understood in the historical and cultural context in which it occurred. It was against the law for a Jewish man to speak with a Gentile woman. Jesus is traveling with his disciples and they are anxious to send away this woman who is begging Jesus to heal her daughter. The law dictated that Jesus have nothing to do with her. She is a Canaanite who worships idols. Any contact with her is forbidden. Jesus ignores his disciples and the prohibition, and challenges her motivation for insisting on his help. There is a clever exchange in which the woman supports her right to receive mercy for her daughter. Jesus praises her faith before the disciples. This woman is both desperate to receive help for her daughter and believes sincerely that Jesus is capable of healing her daughter. There are several interesting insights into Jesus' actions in this unsettling narrative. Even people outside of Israel had heard of the miracles of Jesus. This woman was convinced of Jesus' power by his reputation to heal before she met him. Jesus rebuked his disciples for trying to restrict him from conversing with this foreign woman. Jesus tested this woman's resolve and was impressed with her humility and perseverance. Jesus held her up as an example to the disciples of how they should interact with foreign women. The accepted boundaries of behavior toward women are shattered by Jesus. Her simple faith in Jesus' ability to heal her daughter qualified her for Jesus to perform a miracle of healing. Cultural and religious differences are not an obstacle to Jesus. How disappointing it is that different Christian denominations are hostile to one another, and treat people of other faiths with contempt. Jesus shows us his willingness to respond to anyone of faith who seeks wholeness and deliverance from evil. Mother Theresa spent a lifetime ministering to people of different faiths in India. She treated people with the love and mercy Jesus showed regardless of their religion.

The Woman with the Jar of Ointment
In the Gospel of Luke 7:36-50, we read about Jesus eating in the home of a Pharisee named Simon. A woman enters uninvited to see Jesus and is recognized as a woman of ill repute by the Pharisee. She washes Jesus' feet with her tears, she dries his feet with her hair, she kisses his feet, and she anoints Jesus with the expensive ointment she brought with her. This act of devotion is perceived as scandalous to Simon, and Jesus objects. Jesus tells Simon a parable about forgiveness. Jesus then compares these acts of devotion to the lack of common hospitality that Simon showed Jesus. In Luke 7:44-48 (NRSV), "Then turning toward the woman, he said to Simon, 'Do you see this woman? I entered your house; you gave me no water for my feet, but she has bathed my feet with her tears and dried them with her hair. You gave me no kiss, but from the time I came in she has not stopped kissing my feet. You did not anoint my head with oil, but she has anointed my feet with ointment. Therefore, I tell you, her sins, which were many, have been forgiven; hence she has shown great love. But the one to whom little is forgiven, loves little.' Then he said to her, 'Your sins are forgiven.'"

There is something almost shocking about the graphic display of love and devotion this woman showed to Jesus. It was outside of custom and undignified. This would have been most disturbing to Simon. Even more disturbing was Jesus allowing this woman "of the streets" to touch and kiss his feet. No Pharisee would have any contact with a woman like this. Jesus justifies her with a parable, and compares her actions to Simon's rudeness. Then Jesus forgives her sins and sends her in peace. This is all the more scandalous to Simon because he believes only God can forgive sins. This is the model of how we are to meet sinners who would like to see Jesus. We are to be tolerant of outward displays of emotion. We are to be nonjudgmental even when we are well aware of a person's faults. We are to encourage them into the forgiveness of Jesus and not put obstacles in their way. Jesus was far more interested in this woman's future than he was of her past. Jesus sent her out into the world a new person, with new possibilities for her life. Simon had nothing but contempt for her. This demonstrates the hope for salvation we can offer all people through faith in Jesus. In Matthew 7:1 (NRSV), Jesus said, "Do not judge, so that you may not be judged."

The Samaritan Woman

The first evangelist in the New Testament was the most unlikely candidate for the position. She was not a candidate for being an evangelist, because of her sex, her religion, her morality, and her unbelief. By any reasonable evaluation, she was unqualified to be an evangelist. Women could not give testimony in court because they were women and had no standing. She was a Samaritan and was considered by the Jews to be despicable because of her idolatrous faith. She had been married five times and was living with a man she was not married to. She had no idea who Jesus was and failed to understand his explanation of himself. Jesus chose her to reveal himself to as the Messiah, and by her testimony, many in her village came to believe in Jesus. She was the first evangelist and one cannot imagine a more unlikely candidate for the honor. That is the explanation of why Jesus chose her. Jesus chooses individuals like you and me to be his evangelists.

In the Gospel of John 4:7-26 (NRSV), "A Samaritan woman came to draw water, and Jesus said to her, 'Give me a drink.' (His disciples had gone to the city to buy food.) The Samaritan woman said to him, 'How is it that you, a Jew, ask a drink of me, a woman of Samaria?' (Jews do not share things in common with Samaritans.) Jesus answered her, 'If you knew the gift of God, and who it is that is saying to you, 'Give me a drink,' you would have asked him, and he would have given you living water.' The woman said to him, 'Sir, you have no bucket, and the well is deep. Where do you get that living water? Are you greater than our ancestor Jacob, who gave us the well, and with his sons and his flocks drank from it?' Jesus said to her, 'Everyone who drinks of this water will be thirsty again, but those who drink of the water that I will give them will never be thirsty. The water that I will give will become in them a spring of water gushing up to eternal life.' The woman said to him, 'Sir, give me this water, so that I may never be thirsty or have to keep coming here to draw water.' Jesus said to her, 'Go, call your husband, and come back.' The woman answered him, 'I have no husband.' Jesus said to her, 'You are right in saying, "I have no husband"; for you have had five husbands, and the one you have now is not your husband. What you have said is true!' The woman said to him, 'Sir, I see that you are a prophet. Our ancestors worshiped on this mountain, but you say that the place where people must worship is in Jerusalem.' Jesus said to her, 'Woman, believe me, the hour is coming when you will worship the Father neither on this mountain nor in Jerusalem. You worship what you do not know; we worship what we know, for salvation is from the Jews. But the hour is coming, and is now here, when the true worshipers will worship the Father in spirit and truth, for the Father seeks such as these to worship him. God is spirit, and those who worship him must worship in spirit and truth.' The woman said to him, 'I know that Messiah is coming' (who is called Christ). 'When he comes, he will proclaim all things to us.' Jesus said to her, 'I am he, the one who is speaking to you.'"

This woman went to her village of Sychar and proclaimed she had met a prophet that may be the Messiah. This proclamation aroused the interest in many who went to see Jesus. Many of those came to faith in Jesus. This is a model for evangelism for us today. Tell people of your personal experience of Jesus and then invite them to see for themselves.

Mary Magdalene

The death and resurrection of Jesus is the single most important event in Christianity. The first person to discover that Jesus was raised from the dead was a woman who had also stood at the foot of the cross when Jesus died. The first person to witness to others that Christ had risen from the dead was this same woman, Mary Magdalene. The significance of choosing a woman to be the first witness to the resurrection is extraordinary. This causes us to re-examine our assumptions of the role of women in the church. Throughout history, the importance of the role of women in the Christian faith has been minimized, distorted, and deleted. It is time to restore women to the full participation in the church that Jesus established in the beginning of the faith. Mary Magdalene had been a follower of Jesus and was one of his closest disciples. There are remains of ancient churches in the Middle East that bear the inscriptions they were founded by Mary Magdalene the Apostle of Jesus Christ.

In John 20:1-10 (NRSV), "Early on the first day of the week, while it was still dark, Mary Magdalene came to the tomb and saw that the stone had been removed from the tomb. So she ran and went to Simon Peter and the other disciple, the one whom Jesus loved, and said to them, 'They have taken the Lord out of the tomb, and we do not know where they have laid him.' Then Peter and the other disciple set out and went toward the tomb. The two were running together, but the other disciple outran Peter and reached the tomb first. He bent down to look in and saw the linen wrappings lying there, but he did not go in. Then Simon Peter came, following him, and went into the tomb. He saw the linen wrappings lying there, and the cloth that had been on Jesus' head, not lying with the linen wrappings but rolled up in a place by itself. Then the other disciple, who reached the tomb first, also went in, and he saw and believed; for as yet they did not understand the scripture, that he must rise from the dead. Then the disciples returned to their homes."

After the disciples left the tomb, Mary stayed and had an encounter with the risen Christ. She was weeping and her eyes were filled with tears. She turned around from the darkened tomb and looked into the daylight, and there was a man standing before her. She didn't recognize him through her tears in the bright light. He addressed her and she knew immediately it was Jesus. She attempted to cling to him. Jesus told her to go and tell the Disciples she had seen the Lord. This is the defining moment of Christianity. "The Lord has risen," we say on Easter morning. Mary announced this to the disciples.

Mary has recently been discovered as a major disciple in the early church. There have been the remains of churches that were dedicated to her. We have discovered ancient text that tells of her importance as a disciple of Jesus. There has even been a recent scandal based on a forged fragment that Jesus and Mary Magdalene were married. Mary Magdalene was healed by Jesus of demonic oppression. She has never been identified as a prostitute, but that slander was propagated for centuries to diminish her importance. She is becoming more studied and revered as women assert their rightful roles in the church. Mary Magdalene is one of the greatest figures in the Christian tradition. She must be revered.

In John 20:11-18 (NRSV), "But Mary stood weeping outside the tomb. As she wept, she bent over to look into the tomb; and she saw two angels in white, sitting where the body of Jesus had been lying, one at the head and the other at the feet. They said to her, 'Woman, why are you weeping?' She said to them, 'They have taken away my Lord, and I do not know where they have laid him.' When she had said this, she turned around and saw Jesus standing there, but she did not know that it was Jesus. Jesus said to her, 'Woman, why are you weeping? Whom are you looking for?' Supposing him to be the gardener, she said to him, 'Sir, if you have carried him away, tell me where you have laid him, and I will take him away.' Jesus said to her, 'Mary!' She turned and said to him in Hebrew, 'Rabbouni!'

(which means Teacher). Jesus said to her, 'Do not hold on to me, because I have not yet ascended to the Father. But go to my brothers and say to them, "I am ascending to my Father and your Father, to my God and your God."' Mary Magdalene went and announced to the disciples, 'I have seen the Lord'; and she told them that he had said these things to her."

Mary announced the resurrection of Jesus to the Disciples. This witness of the resurrection changes the understanding of who Jesus was. He is more than a prophet, more than a healer, more than a miracle worker, more than an enlightened teacher, and more than his Disciples imagined. Jesus is truly the Son of God. When Mary said, "I have seen the Lord," she was stating a fact that changed the world. If Jesus had died and was buried in the tomb, that would have been the end of the Jesus movement. The resurrection is the beginning of the Jesus movement which became known as Christianity. The faith of Mary Magdalene is where it begins for us. The Disciples all had experiences of the bodily resurrection of Jesus just as Mary did. Later, Paul had an experience of the risen Lord on the road to Damascus which changed the movement to include Gentiles. Almost all Biblical scholars agree that these reports are genuine historical events. Millions of people over the past two thousand years have had encounters with the risen Christ. These are testimonies to the truth which Mary Magdalene first reported.

CHAPTER 9
HIS COMMANDMENTS

The Ten Commandments are recorded in Exodus 20:2-17 (NRSV). Jesus stated that we must obey these commandments and he preached on them. He summarized these commandments in one simple commandment: "I give you a new commandment, that you love one another. Just as I have loved you, you also should love one another," John 13:34 (NRSV). Jesus devoted much of his teaching and actions demonstrating how the Ten Commandments are fulfilled both by our actions and by our love. Jesus was teaching the essential truth of the Ten Commandments by refining them to their essential truth. We are to love in thought, word, and deed.

Jesus was asked which was the greatest commandment. He replied, "'You shall love the Lord your God with all your heart, and with all your soul, and with all your mind.' This is the greatest and first commandment. And a second is like it: 'You shall love your neighbor as yourself,'" Matthew 22:37-39 (NRSV). This clearly explains how Jesus understood the entire law was dependent upon love. Jesus was completely consistent in his teaching of the law, and specific about how the law must be internalized as well as external application. Jesus neither changed the law nor selectively applied it. Rather, Jesus both vigorously supported the Jewish law as it had been written in the Torah for over a thousand years, and he amplified its meaning. There is clearly reference to the Ten Commandments as the "law" as the most important law. Jews and Christians would agree the Ten Commandments are the essential laws. The different Jewish and Christian paths would disagree about the contemporary relevance of all the other laws contained in the Hebrew Scriptures. There are "light and heavy" laws in the Torah. The important point is that Jesus' upholding of the Ten Commandments is what the Judeo-Christian faiths have believed from the beginning and continue to believe. These are held as universal and absolute truths.

1

The first commandment states, "I am the LORD your God, who brought you out of the land of Egypt, out of the house of slavery; you shall have no other gods before me," Exodus 20:2-3 (NRSV). At the time this commandment was given, the world was pantheistic. The concept of one God was unknown. Monotheism was a radical concept that was a threat to the pantheistic religions of the times. The pantheistic Romans accused the Jews and Christians of being atheists because they refused to acknowledge the gods of Rome as deities. The clashes of religions, in the ancient world, were about whose gods were stronger and would dominate. The idea of monotheism was a fundamental challenge to pantheism. Religion was an expression of tribalism. Monotheism is universal. In fact, the monotheist viewed the worship of many gods as demonic. The first commandment is unequivocal about the singular and complete God. The prohibition of worship of other gods is definitive. There are some references in the Scriptures to other gods, but they are not to be worshipped. The second commandment elaborates on this theme.

2

The second commandment states, "You shall not make for yourself an idol, whether in the form of anything that is in heaven above, or that is on the earth beneath, or that is in the water under the earth. You shall not bow down to them or worship them; for I the LORD your God am a jealous God, punishing children for the iniquity of parents, to the third and the fourth generation of those who reject me, but showing steadfast love to the thousandth generation of those who love me and keep my commandments," Exodus 20:4-6 (NRSV). An idol is an object of worship and the critical meaning is the word worship. To prevent even the possibility of worship, this has at times included the prohibition of any imagery other than abstractions for decorative purposes. The more liberal understanding is that imagery is not prohibited as long as it is not used for worship. Christians have been using images from their earliest beginnings as instructional and devotional guides, but insist these images are not worshiped. Chartres Cathedral, built in the eleven hundreds, was one of the first universities in the world. The walls and windows are a systematic and comprehensive illustration of the Holy Bible using thousands of images. The lecturers used these images in stone and stained glass to educate students. Books were extremely rare and expensive. The Cathedral was the Biblical knowledge displayed for all to benefit from. During the Protestant reformation, iconoclasts destroyed the images in the churches in the belief that images could be mistakenly worshipped in violation of the second commandment. There was also a flourishing trade amongst Protestants in lurid illustrations of the demonic images at work. So imagery was not condemned, only devotional images that were venerated.

    The part of the second commandment that is not controversial is about God's "steadfast love to the thousandth generation of those who love me and keep my commandments." The absolute primacy of loving God and keeping his commandments is what Jesus focused upon. In the modern world, we would deny the notion of idols, but is this true? Do we have idols that we worship and pretend they are not worshipped? An argument could be made that we have many transitory idols in our culture such as celebrities, possessions, and customs. This begs the question of how we understand worship. Jesus challenged people of his day to consider these questions. He questioned the prohibition of gathering grain to eat on the Sabbath. He questioned capital punishment for women caught in adultery. He questioned association with sinners. He questioned the marketing of worship at the temple in Jerusalem. These examples are specific issues that can be understood as idolatry in different forms. How do we make our religious practices idolatry? This is a subject that requires rigorous self-examination and constant vigilance. This is why Jesus stresses the importance of internalizing the love basis for the commandments, rather than just strict obedience to the external application of the laws.

3
The third commandment states, "You shall not make wrongful use of the name of the LORD your God, for the LORD will not acquit anyone who misuses his name," Exodus 20:7 (NRSV). This commandment should be understood but it is apparently neither appreciated nor obeyed even by Christians. To put this commandment into common language, it states, do not misuse the knowing or the use of God. Blasphemy is trash talking the name of God, but it is more than that. Blasphemy is abusing the knowledge of God. We must not use God's name as a curse, an exclamation, a condemnation, or in any irreverent way. Further, the misuse of the knowing of God must not be used to misrepresent God. It is an abuse of the name of God to solicit money for God's favors. It is an abuse of the knowing of God to demonize others who have a differing theological understanding (unless the practices are harmful to others). It is an abuse of the third commandment to acquire power and control over others for personal gain. These violations of the third commandment are unfortunately all too common. In examining the life of Jesus recorded in the Gospels, he never approached exploiting his divinity or his power for gain.

The disturbing quality of Jesus was his humility and complete absence of desire for power, possessions, or domination. Jesus allows us to freely pursue our every impulse and loves us even when we rebel against him. Jesus disapproves of unrighteous behavior but will forgive us when we have gone astray. Like the sheep that has gone astray, we are welcomed back when we are found. No matter how bad we behave, we are always received back in love. Because of his love for us, we need to live holding the name of God in reverence. In living a life that is not misusing our knowledge of God, we must never exploit that relationship with God in any way. There have been too many individuals who have successfully achieved power, wealth, and fame by exploiting the name of God. This is not only going to have dire consequences on their fate, but it has discouraged trust in God by people who have witnessed this corruption of faith.

A surprising part of the revelation of God in the Bible is the emotional character of God. How much of these emotions are the anthropomorphisms attributed to God are how much is true revelation is debatable. The revelation of God's true nature in the person of Jesus Christ shows us the range of emotions of God. Misuse of God is taken very seriously by Jesus in the Scriptures. The only times we see Jesus truly angry is when the name of God is misused. The Pharisees are castigated by Jesus for being hypocrites. They are misusing the knowledge of God with oppressive rules and self-promotion. Jesus is angry about the abuses of the temple, money changers, and sellers of sacrificial animals for profit. Jesus warns us against the sin of blasphemy against the Holy Spirit. This is the Spirit of God and also known as the Spirit of Truth. The reason why he tells us this is unforgivable is because when we intentionally distort the truth, we have alienated ourselves from truth. Repentance and forgiveness are difficult to recover when we have lost the foundation of truth. Lies not only destroy the fabric of society; they destroy the foundation of the soul. How difficult, if not impossible, it is for an intentional web of lies to be recoverable back into honesty and trust.

4
The fourth commandment states, "Remember the Sabbath day, and keep it holy. Six days you shall labor and do all your work. But the seventh day is a Sabbath to the LORD your God; you shall not do any work—you, your son or your daughter, your male or female slave, your livestock, or the alien resident in your towns. For in six days the LORD made heaven and earth, the sea, and all that is in them, but rested the seventh day; therefore the LORD blessed the Sabbath day and consecrated it," Exodus 20:8-11 (NRSV).

This commandment has been reinterpreted by most Christians. Practicing Jews take it seriously and observe the Sabbath. It has become the custom for Christians to observe the Sabbath on Sunday the first day of the week. There are several reasons why the Sabbath was changed from Saturday to Sunday. It is not important to review the rationales for this change in this book about Jesus. The issue that is relevant is taking a day of rest once a week and consecrating that day to God. As a clergy person, our Sundays are not a day of rest and we work on that day. Many clergy take another day during the week as a rest day. How one defines rest varies widely, but an absence of work would be part of the definition. The important decision is to have the day of rest and set aside that day for strengthening one's relationship with God.

5
The fifth commandment states, "Honor your father and your mother, so that your days may be long in the land that the LORD your God is giving you," Exodus 20:12 (NRSV). This commandment seems so fundamental but, in reality, family relations can be so complicated and become dysfunctional. The commandment firmly places the responsibility for family prosperity on the

offspring. All parents are flawed human beings. Their children must honor their parents regardless of their faults. There might be an exception to this if the parents are destructive people and the welfare of the children would be harmed by interaction with the parents. This is very rare and could be the reverse situation where the children are harmful. Jesus warned that families may be torn apart by following Jesus. The offspring have a duty to honor, respect, and care for their parents. In contemporary society, the placing of parents in nursing homes or residential communities has become common. Sadly, it is not uncommon for the parent to be abandoned in these situations. If you talk to the residents in these homes, the biggest complaint is neglect by their families. This is both an injustice to the parent and an insult to God. Many older people dread the day they will be abandoned in an old people's home. In developing countries, there are no old people's homes and the family cares for the elderly, and the elderly participate in the life of the family as much as possible. Jesus cared for his mother even when he was dying on the cross.

6

The sixth commandment states, "You shall not murder," Exodus 20:13 (NRSV). Jesus calls us to address the root cause of murder in the Sermon on the Mount. In Matthew 5:22 (NRSV), "But I say to you that if you are angry with a brother or sister, you will be liable to judgment." He then added the insult of calling someone a fool which was a terrible smear in his day. Everyone gets angry at times whether it is justified or not. Jesus tells us to quickly be reconciled with the person you are having conflict with. It is not sufficient that we not commit murder. Jesus demands that we seek reconciliation with everyone. That can mean a variety of things. This may result in repairing a friendship or it may mean separation for an indeterminate period of time. Every situation is going to have a unique outcome. The objective is to eliminate anger and the hurt of insults. Jesus gives us lessons on how to love our enemies by responding with love. This is interesting because the commandment by Jesus is to not seek revenge, justice, or equivalency. We are told by Jesus to love our enemies. This may be the hardest commandment of them all because it goes go directly against human nature. Is this possible? What would be the cost of loving our enemy as opposed to battling our enemy? Can we defend ourselves? Jesus tells his disciples to carry a sword, so that must be for self-defense. What does loving your enemy look like? Are humans capable of settling their differences with reason and making compromise? When reason and compromise fail, what do we do? The answers to all these questions are speculation until we are confronted with a real situation and then they become matters of serious consideration. With the help of God, we can be successful in loving our enemy.

7

The seventh commandment states, "You shall not commit adultery," Exodus 20:14 (NRSV). Jesus opposed the execution of women caught in adultery which was the law of the Hebrew Testament. Jesus addressed the problem of adultery by confronting men with the responsibility for adultery. This was a radical approach. Has there ever existed a man who has not had lustful thoughts about a woman? Most men confess to struggling with many lustful thoughts. Jesus proclaims these very thoughts as equivalent to the commission of adultery. Therefore, most if not all men have broken this commandment. The purpose of Jesus is not the condemnation of men; rather, he is showing the way for men to avoid being adulterers in thought, word, and deed. The fact is we can control our thoughts. We are capable of changing our minds if we so choose. This is a matter of motivation and practice. Mankind does not have to be a slave to the bestial instincts. There are numerous examples of men and women who have behaved in the manner that Jesus described. The power of the Holy Spirit has the ability to transform a person if they desire that change. We are in this world to be sanctified, if we desire this transformation. Jesus wants men to view women with dignity and respect, and not as sex objects.

8

The eighth commandment states, "You shall not steal," Exodus 20:15 (NRSV). Jesus teaches a gospel of sharing, so stealing would be contrary to the spirit of sharing. Jesus told his disciples if you are asked for something, give them more. If you are asked to do something, do more than they ask. Stealing destroys the social order. Jesus' spirit of generosity builds a new social order. Stealing obliterates trust and Jesus is all about building trust.

9

The ninth commandment states, "You shall not bear false witness against your neighbor," Exodus 20:16 (NRSV). There is an interesting exchange between Jesus and the Pharisees in the Gospel of John 8:12-59. Jesus is explaining himself to these men and they are accusing him of everything they can think to say. They even accuse Jesus of having a demon. At the end of the disagreement, the Pharisees picked up stones to kill Jesus, but he hid himself and withdrew. False witness is lying about someone. Jesus said to the Pharisees, "When he lies, he speaks according to his own nature, for he is a liar and the father of lies," John 8:44 (NRSV). The opposition to God has no regard for the truth and will say anything. This is a powerful condemnation of the liar, one who bears false witness.

10

The tenth commandment states, "You shall not covet your neighbor's house; you shall not covet your neighbor's wife, or male or female slave, or ox, or donkey, or anything that belongs to your neighbor," Exodus 20:17 (NRSV). The consumer economy is based on creating desire for more and more. The vast majority of Americans have more of everything than they need. No one is ever satisfied with what they have because they crave more of anything and everything. We covet it all. Because we are insatiable, the coveting only increases like a cancer. How have we allowed ourselves to become slaves to consumerism? Jesus spoke often about our material needs. In Luke 12:15 (NRSV), Jesus said, "Take care! Be on your guard against all kinds of greed; for one's life does not consist in the abundance of possessions." He follows this statement with a chilling parable that warns against "those who store up treasures for themselves but are not rich toward God," Luke 12:21 (NRSV). Many Americans may not be concerned about the poverty in the world because they feel threatened that charity and equitable distribution of resources may hinder their acquisition of more goods. Our nation is a nation of hoarders.

The Hope and Despair in the Law

As we study the law and take it seriously, we are increasingly convicted of our sinfulness. How can there be any good weighted against the sins we commit? We may attempt to justify ourselves by defining the law on a superficial level. I never murder anyone. I never stole from anyone. I never had sex with another person outside of marriage. And we go through the Ten Commandments and claim our innocence. Saint Paul explains this relation of law to salvation in his letter to the Romans beautifully. Thinking we can justify ourselves under the law is self-deception. If we listen to Jesus, we are guilty of breaking the laws if we entertained in our thoughts the prohibited actions. Who dares say they are innocent after a scrupulous self-examination. The law brings us to an awareness of our depravity.

The law is good because it makes us conscious of who we really are and drives us to seek a way to salvation. The good news is there is a way to salvation, and that is not scrambling for some imaginary self-justification. The way of salvation is the Savior Jesus who takes our sin upon himself so that we may be justified before God. Jesus not only takes away the sin of the world, but he also gives us the means to become holy people. He sends the Holy Spirit upon, with, and throughout us to abide with us to transform us from sinners into saints. This process of transformation is slow and takes constant effort on our part. It is the battle of a lifetime, but it is the work we were born to do in this world. We will be easily defeated in this struggle if we depend on magical thinking. There are times when God gives us progress in miraculous ways, and there are other struggles where God allows us to fight the good fight over years. One of the biggest enemies of our success is discouragement. This is the slow erosion of our faith in God's ability to be victorious. The God who made the universe will be victorious. This is the underlying message of the Bible. God wins. By the power of the Holy Spirit, and with our cooperation, we win. This little life is a drama of peaks and valleys. Through the failures and successes, we are transformed into the beings that we were created to be before we were born. God did not make us to be failures. God did not make us to go to hell. God made us to be radiant saints in heaven and on earth. God has given us everything we need by the Holy Scriptures, by the church, by the company of the saints in process, by the power of prayer, by the indwelling Holy Spirit, and by the grace of our Savior Jesus. With these instruments, we will find sanctification. We will find our justification. We will find our salvation. Thankfully, we have the law which is the beginning of our journey from the life of sin towards redemption.

CHAPTER 10
HIS PROMISE

Jesus made numerous extraordinary promises to his disciples that are recorded in the Gospels and these are given to us. The most life changing promise he made concerns our eternal destiny. He has promised eternal life in heaven to those who believe in him and follow his way. There is no comparable promise in the entire world. To believe and follow should be the same thing, because if you believe in him you would follow him; conversely, if you do not follow him you do not believe in him. Human beings are masters of self-deception, so let us not fool ourselves by being counterfeit Christians. The Bible says you shall know them by their fruits. Do the lives we lead bear the fruits of Christ? If the answer is yes, then that is the affirmation that we need to know that our faith is genuine, and we can be assured his promises apply to us.

Jesus tells us that he is going to heaven to prepare a place for us. Humans are not divine beings; neither are they immortal. Humans are frail and deeply flawed creatures, which are being raised up from their natural state into a spiritual state. We have the potential to become Christ-like beings, but only through the transformation of our natural self. This process of transformation is to perfect us as beings who belong in heaven, and it is a long and difficult process of purification. Only the pure in heart will see the face of God, and we must be perfected or purified in order to come into the presence of God. Jesus has gone ahead of us to prepare a place for us where we will be perfected as part of our transformation into Christ-like beings. In John 14:1-3 (NRSV), Jesus said, "Do not let your hearts be troubled. Believe in God, believe also in me. In my Father's house there are many dwelling places. If it were not so, would I have told you that I go to prepare a place for you? And if I go and prepare a place for you, I will come again and will take you to myself, so that where I am, there you may be also." Jesus promises us that he will come for us and take us to heaven to be with him. Jesus is our Savior because he teaches us the way to heaven, he has prepared a place for us in heaven, he shows us the way to heaven, he takes us to heaven, and he perfects us in heaven. He has taken our sins upon himself so that we are justified before God. The only thing he will not do is force someone to go with him. We have to respond to his invitation to trust him and follow him or we don't go with him.

He goes ahead of us and prepares a place for us, and he will take us there. Once a person understands what Jesus is promising, it is difficult to comprehend why anyone would refuse him. And that is the test that determines whether a person goes to heaven or not. If a person has the desire to be with God, they would grasp at the opportunity to be with God by any Godly means possible. Any rational assessment of the human character knows that we are unholy beings not worthy of being in God's presence, and only through the intercession of a Savior could we ever hope to come into the presence of God. Jesus offers us this opportunity with the only condition that we trust in him and follow the way of love. If we do this, he will take us to heaven and perfect us so that we might come into the presence of God. A person who rejects this invitation evidently is not interested in coming into the presence of God. Jesus makes it emphatically clear that this is our chance, and to reject it has grave consequences.

If we love Jesus, we will obey his commandments. In John 14:21 (NRSV), Jesus tells us, "They who have my commandments and keep them are those who love me." His commandments are not easy and our obedience to his commandments do not come naturally. It is a continuous struggle between the bestial nature of humans and our transformation into Christ-like beings. Because Jesus came to us in human form, he understands the struggle between our worldly nature and our spiritual nature. He is patient with us, and never gives us more than we can bear. When we are in the struggle of the old self becoming the Christ-like person, we will experience suffering of different kinds, for this is a byproduct of the transforming process. We will face trials and testing in the process. What we must always strive for is obedience to his commandments. Our love is demonstrated by our obedience to him. When we truly love someone, we see their needs as greater than our own. When we love Jesus, we desire his will to be our will. We want his needs and interests to be our needs and interests. We want his love to be our love. As his will becomes greater in our life, our will becomes less, so that the Spirit of Christ is embodied in our life. In this process of transformation, we are becoming one with Jesus, and one with God the Father. In John 14:18-21 (NRSV), Jesus says, "I will not leave you orphaned; I am coming to you. In a little while the world will no longer see me, but you will see me; because I live, you also will live. On that day you will know that I am in my Father, and you in me, and I in you. They who have my commandments and keep them are those who love me; and those who love me will be loved by my Father, and I will love them and reveal myself to them." Our eternal salvation is dependent on our intimacy with Jesus.

Jesus has told us and in the clearest possible language who is going to heaven and who will not go to heaven. He described exactly what will determine whether a person is worthy of going to heaven or is not. It is not the works themselves that makes a person worthy of going to heaven. The evidence of the works shows love and obedience to Jesus which proves a person belongs to Jesus. In Matthew 25:31-34 (NRSV), "When the Son of Man comes in his glory, and all the angels with him, then he will sit on the throne of his glory. All the nations will be gathered before him, and he will separate people one from another as a shepherd separates the sheep from the goats, and he will put the sheep at his right hand and the goats at the left. Then the king will say to those at his right hand, 'Come, you that are blessed by my Father, inherit the kingdom prepared for you from the foundation of the world.'" Jesus spoke to the people of his day in language that they could understand, using illustrations that they could also understand. The overwhelming majority of the population was involved in agriculture, and he often used agricultural illustrations. In his day, shepherds often tended mixed herds of sheep and goats which had to be separated at night. Just as the shepherds sorted his flocks, so will we be sorted according to our love and obedience to Jesus. How we have lived our lives is the judgment of our lives.

Jesus tells us that it is our deeds that are the proof of our faith. If we live a Christ-like life, then we are an obedient follower of Jesus. So that we will not deceive ourselves, Jesus gives us specific examples of what a Christ-like life looks like. These are examples of what Jesus did when he was in this world, and these are activities that he taught his disciples to do as his followers. In Matthew 25:35-40 (NRSV), "'For I was hungry and you gave me food, I was thirsty and you gave me something to drink, I was a stranger and you welcomed me, I was naked and you gave me clothing, I was sick and you took care of me, I was in prison and you visited me.' Then the righteous will answer him, 'Lord, when was it that we saw you hungry and gave you food, or thirsty and gave you something to drink? And when was it that we saw you a stranger and welcomed you, or naked and gave you clothing? And when was it that we saw you sick or in prison and visited you?' And the king will answer them, 'Truly I tell you, just as you did it to one of the least of these who are members of my family, you did it to me.'" Jesus tells us that every act we do is as if we were doing it to him. Since the Spirit of Christ is everywhere, everything we do is done in his presence. The way that we treat our fellow human being is the way that we treat Jesus. The compassion that we show must be like the compassion that he showed us.

Our eternal destination is completely dependent upon whether we have been obedient to the commandments of Christ or not. Human beings can pretend that we are Christians, but God will not be deceived. We may call ourselves Christians, but if we do not live Christ-like lives, we are counterfeit and we will suffer the consequences. Matthew 25:41-46 (NRSV) states, "Then he will say to those at his left hand, 'You that are accursed, depart from me into the eternal fire prepared for the devil and his angels; for I was hungry and you gave me no food, I was thirsty and you gave me nothing to drink, I was a stranger and you did not welcome me, naked and you did not give me clothing, sick and in prison and you did not visit me.' Then they also will answer, 'Lord, when was it that we saw you hungry or thirsty or a stranger or naked or sick or in prison, and did not take care of you?' Then he will answer them, 'Truly I tell you, just as you did not do it to one of the least of these, you did not do it to me.' And these will go away into eternal punishment, but the righteous into eternal life." The only way to heaven is by living a Christ-like life. Anything else is the way to separation from God, which is hell.

Jesus promises the Holy Spirit to guide us on our journey. We are equipped with an inner guidance system. This shepherd's voice keeps us on the right path which is sanctification. Of course, this only works if we pay close attention to the voice and stirrings of the Holy Spirit. The Holy Spirit gives us gifts to equip us for ministry and the Holy Spirit changes our character so that we bear the fruits of the Spirit. The whole purpose of the Holy Spirit is to lead us and the world to Christ who leads us to God. In John 14:16 (NRSV), Jesus informs us, "And I will ask the Father, and he will give you another Advocate, to be with you forever." The Advocate is also called the Holy Spirit, The Spirit of Christ, the Spirit of truth, the counselor; he is our advisor, he is our conscience, and he is our wisdom which surpasses worldly wisdom. In John 14:17 (NRSV), "This is the Spirit of truth, whom the world cannot receive, because it neither sees him nor knows him. You know him, because he abides with you, and he will be in you."

When Jesus tells us that he will always be with us, he is referring to the Holy Spirit which is also his Spirit. This is the critical distinction between knowing Jesus and knowing about Jesus. To know Jesus is to have an ongoing intimate relationship with him. Jesus was a rabbi, prophet, radical, reformer, and divine being. Those are only descriptive facets of who he was. Jesus is a living being that we interact with and who is always with us. Life with Jesus is completely different than life without Jesus. We rely upon him continuously and live to please him. We do not fear our mistakes and sins because he forgives us and is most patient with us. His love is similar to the best friend we could imagine. He also informs us when we have failed and helps us to improve in our decisions. Everything in life is about making choices and he gently guides in making the better choices. We can be duplicitous with him, but he is always honest and trustworthy with us. The more we rely upon him, the more we become dependent upon his counsel.

If the whole world knew life with the living Spirit of Christ in our hearts and minds, this world would be a paradise compared to the reality of the world we have created. The promise of Christ Jesus abiding in the whole of humankind is the will of God as stated in the Holy Scriptures. The second coming is the universal internalization of the Holy Spirit. Too often, there is a focus on the possible catastrophes of the apocalyptic events preceding the second coming. The second coming of Christ is the end of this era in human history and a rebirth into a glorious new era. How and when these world changing events will take place is a mystery, but they are a cause for hope and not fear. It is God's will that all humanity take the next leap forward in our development. With the help of the Holy Spirit, this could be in the form of a great global awakening, a movement of the Spirit unlike anything the world has known is coming. This is what God wants to happen. As long as this rebirth is resisted by us, there will be increasing measures to urge us toward the new world. God's will is unstoppable and inevitable. It is infinitely more rewarding to be participating in God's plan for the expansion of God consciousness than it is to be opposing God. Knowing Jesus Christ and living by his Spirit is both about our personal salvation and, far more importantly, life in Christ is about the salvation of the world. The whole creation is groaning in labor pains for this birth of glory of God on earth as it is in heaven.

CHAPTER 11

PRAYER

Prayer is conversation with God. It is frequently understood to be a one-way conversation, but it is not intended to be exclusively us talking to God, and God remaining silent. That is an immature concept of prayer. Prayer is asking, begging, pleading, and it is more. Prayer is worshipping, honoring, and listening to God. To begin understanding prayer as Jesus taught us, we need to examine what prayer is.

If God knows everything, why do we pray? Since God is omniscient, God knows our prayer before we pray, so why bother? The focusing of our mind on conscious thought is an intentional act, as opposed to the constant stream of thoughts that race through our minds. Science tells us that we have hundreds of thoughts per minute. We think at a much greater rate than we could speak. To concentrate upon something takes effort and selectively organizes our thoughts. To formulate a prayer takes conscious effort and that informs us about what is important to us. God is interested in what we deliberately wish to convey to God as opposed to the stream of consciousness that pours through our minds. Praying also informs us of our relation with God. We put our hopes, desires, fears, and worship for God to examine and for us to examine. Guided by the Holy Spirit, we may be surprised by our prayers. Prayer can also be an opportunity to vent our emotions. Prayer can be very therapeutic. Prayer is a means of sharing the burdens we carry with our Higher Power. Our prayer has two recipients, God and ourselves.

The Best Prayer

Jesus tells us the best prayer is honest, humble, and direct. In Luke 18:9-14 (NRSV), Jesus contrasted the long and self-righteous prayer of a Pharisee with the brief prayer of a sinner, "God, be merciful to me, a sinner!" the tax collector prayed. This is the basis of a prayer that has been used by Christians for two thousand years called the Jesus prayer. There are several variations but they are all essentially the same. One form of this prayer is, "Jesus Christ, Son of God, have mercy upon me for I am a sinner redeemed by your love." This prayer is often repeated several times. For mysterious reasons, the repetition of this prayer causes it to become more heartfelt. Repetition has this effect of deepening prayer rather than devaluing it. The Jesus prayer is appropriate for the praying novice, the intermediate, and the saint. This is a recommendation and should not be understood as an exclusion of all types of prayer. The important point to remember is, stay humble and keep it simple. God is not impressed with flowery language or prideful self-promotion.

When Jesus was asked how we should pray, he gave us the Lord's Prayer, in Matthew 6:9-13 (NRSV). In five short verses, Jesus gave us a model of prayer. This is a short prayer that is quite comprehensive. There are several intriguing dimensions to this prayer. The prayer is from the perspective of the many and not from only one individual. The prayer is from us and not from me, my, or I. Prayer needs to be inclusive and not exclusive. The prayer begins with a specific and reverent address to God. "Our Father in heaven, hallowed be your name," Matthew 6:9 (NRSV). Who are we praying to when we choose to converse with God? The address is important and the honoring God is important. If you think you may throw your desires and hopes out into the universe, you are naïve about the complexity and diversity of the spiritual realm. Address is critical. Humility is critical. The first two verses are specific in these matters.

The second verse ten is fascinating because it states, "Your kingdom come. Your will be done, on earth as it is in heaven," Matthew 6:10 (NRSV). Are we telling God something God is unaware of? That is absurd, so it must mean something else. It means we are in one accord with God about the will of God becoming universal in this world. We are stating our agreement for the necessity of God's will in this world. This has profound implications for us and everyone on the planet. If this were to come about, the world would be radically changed. We would barely recognize our planet. The second verse of the Lord's Prayer invites us to be a participant in God's plan of salvation. Welcome to the ministry and mission following Jesus Christ.

The third verse of the Lord's Prayer states, "Give us this day our daily bread," Matthew 6:11 (NRSV). This is both specific and symbolic of all our human needs. Bread was the staple of life in ancient times. It can be understood to represent everything we need to sustain us in life. Jesus tells us that God will give us everything we need for life. Jesus never implies we will have more than we need. It is possible to pray for more than is necessary, but it is insulting to God for us to display our greed and envy. There is another understanding of the bread we are asking for in this prayer. Jesus is the bread of life and we are offered this bread in the Holy Communion. This deepens our request for the daily bread because it suggests we are asking for the bread of Jesus. This takes us to a wholly new level of prayer in this seemingly humble request.

The fourth verse states, "And forgive us our debts, as we also have forgiven our debtors," Matthew 6:12 (NRSV). This has been expressed in the Scriptures as we forgive so shall we be forgiven. We are forced to face how we have forgiven if we hope to be forgiven. Another approach to this is, as we are forgiven so we should forgive. We who are forgiven much (which is everyone who has received Christ Jesus' total forgiveness by his death on the cross) must respond by forgiving everyone completely. Jesus elaborates on this subject in Matthew 7:1-5, in teaching about judging others. How hard it is for us to let it go. We cling to resentments and withholding forgiveness. Often it is only by the power of the Holy Spirit are we capable of forgiving. This is one of those problem areas in life we must rely upon the help of God.

The fifth verse is, "And do not bring us to the time of trial, but rescue us from the evil one," Matthew 6:13 (NRSV). God does not test us. God does allow us to be tested. This is an important distinction. Too often, people accuse God of the problems in their lives. This is dangerous ground and will lead to separation from God if not corrected. Besides our own flawed selves, and the nature of the physical world, there is an entity who does nothing but test us. Jesus identifies it as the evil one, also known as the prince of darkness, and satan. This is the adversary of God which is what the word satan means in Greek. It is unfortunate that this word is used as a proper noun because it is a description more than a title. Jesus uses this word to admonish his disciple Peter. The adversary of God is always working on us to test us. What is the purpose of this testing? Testing is a trial or examination to determine the true character of a person. In education, tests are used to help the student objectively know what knowledge they have acquired in a specific field. Testing is not the sadistic urges of the teacher to create anxiety in students. The importance of tests is what the individual learns from them. Everyone is tested and some more than others. It is not for us to know why some are tested more than others. God knows why. The amazing reality of humans is that some succeed at passing the tests with honors and others fail and succumb to evil at the most rudimentary testing.

There are saintly people who are tested with ordeals that are disturbing to imagine. Some of these people are martyrs who did not deserve the torments that were inflicted upon them. Others are people all around us going through ordeals of horrible incurable diseases, oppressive social systems, and crushing poverty. Why do they suffer? God knows, and we have the choice to help them in their suffering or ignore them. Mostly we ignore suffering in the world because it is so threatening to us, and we feel helpless engaging in the suffering of others. When we pray the Lord's Prayer, we are praying not only for ourselves. We are praying for the world. The Lord's Prayer encourages us to become involved in the trials of all people. Jesus did not fix all the problems of the world, but he did respond to the people in need in their circumstances. This is all he asks of us. He gives us a few specific ways we can help those who are going through trials in Matthew 25, and he says he will determine our sincerity and devotion to him by our involvement with our sisters and brothers on this journey.

Power of Prayer
Jesus says there is no limit to what can be achieved if we had sufficient faith and prayed. To anyone who has had their prayers denied, this proves we do not have the kind of faith Jesus was specifying we needed.

Where is this faith and how do we get the power to move mountains? In Mark 11:22-24 (NRSV), Jesus says, "Have faith in God. Truly I tell you, if you say to this mountain, 'Be taken up and thrown into the sea,' and if you do not doubt in your heart, but believe that what you say will come to pass, it will be done for you. So I tell you, whatever you ask for in prayer, believe that you have received it, and it will be yours." This passage is very disturbing to many of us because we have failed in prayer frequently. We think we have faith. Evidently, our faith is not what we imagine or it is not yet the time for such miracles of faith. In the future, when the Spirit of Christ reigns in every heart, this scripture will be universally true. In our present world of faithlessness and doubt, this scripture cannot be realized. Even Jesus could do no miracles in the environment of unbelief. See Mark 6:5 when Jesus was rejected in his hometown. The power of prayer depends not only upon the faith of the individual, but also upon the whole environment of faith. Corporate prayer unleashes some of the power of prayer. What if we united the Christian community in prayer? What would united Christians be capable of doing?

<u>Persistence in Prayer</u>
Jesus wants us to be persistent in our prayers. He understands our human nature better than we do, which is why he knows that we must be persistent in our prayer. He told a powerful story to illustrate his point. In Luke 11:5-8 (NRSV), "Suppose one of you has a friend, and you go to him at midnight and say to him, 'Friend, lend me three loaves of bread; for a friend of mine has arrived, and I have nothing to set before him.' And he answers from within, 'Do not bother me; the door has already been locked, and my children are with me in bed; I cannot get up and give you anything.' I tell you, even though he will not get up and give him anything because he is his friend, at least because of his persistence he will get up and give him whatever he needs."

The truth that this parable is teaching us is that we must be persistent in our prayer in order to get what we need, which is to conform ourselves to the will of God. God knows what we need before we even ask, and wants to give us that which will make us more Christ-like. Our persistent prayer is necessary for us to ask, seek, and knock on the door for the right thing according to our need.

The Spirit of Christ will even inspire us to say what needs to be said at the right time in the right place when we put our trust in God. When in doubt, and even when you are not in doubt, ask the indwelling Spirit of God to give you the words to speak, and you will find precisely the right thing say. Jesus is always there for you to give you what you need. In Luke 12:11-12 (NRSV), "When they bring you before the synagogues, the rulers, and the authorities, do not worry about how you are to defend yourselves or what you are to say; for the Holy Spirit will teach you at that very hour what you ought to say." Let God be the God of your heart, mind, and soul.

Prayer is the Connection
Jesus Christ is the perfect revelation of God so humans can know God and approach the throne of grace. Jesus knows the human experience and empathizes with us. He invites us to come to him, know him, to love him, and to live in him. In Matthew 11:28-30 (NRSV), "Come to me, all you that are weary and are carrying heavy burdens, and I will give you rest. Take my yoke upon you, and learn from me; for I am gentle and humble in heart, and you will find rest for your souls. For my yoke is easy, and my burden is light." We find in our intimate relationship with Jesus the peace that surpasses all understanding. In our prayer with Jesus, we will receive all the good gifts that he wants to give us, and we will not receive those things that we ask for which we do not need. We do not know God's perfect plan or will for us, but Jesus does know because he is one with God. When we pray, sometimes the answer is yes, sometimes the answer is no, and sometimes the answer is maybe later. This is how we respond to our children. No good parent gives their children everything they ask for. Through prayer, we learn and grow to become more like Jesus, living in obedience to God. We do not pray to make God do what we want. We pray to learn what God wants us to do. Our prayers are from an infant speaking to the parent. God requires honesty above all else. Prayer based on hypocrisy or meaningless babble has no interest to God and gains us nothing. The only right way to pray is from the heart.

The Spirit of Christ abides in the very core of our being, which is what it means to pray from the heart. When we pray from the heart, we are speaking from and listening to the Spirit of Christ that lives in us. The Spirit knows what we should pray for and what we need. In Romans 8:26-27 (NRSV), "Likewise the Spirit helps us in our weakness; for we do not know how to pray as we ought, but that very Spirit intercedes with sighs too deep for words. And

God, who searches the heart, knows what is the mind of the Spirit, because the Spirit intercedes for the saints according to the will of God." Fruitful prayer is to become harmonious with the will of God. We were given this life experience to glorify God by learning and doing God's will. Prayer is the immediate connection between ourselves and God. Prayer is entering into a sacred relationship with God and should be so treated.

God knows everything, and knows what we want and what we need before we even ask. If we are asking for what we need, we will be given; if we are searching for the truth, we will find what we seek; and if we are looking for the opportunity to serve God, the opening will appear. Jesus implores us to go for it. He tells us to ask, seek, and knock. When we strive for the good gifts that he wants to give us we, will receive them. In Matthew 7:7-11 (NRSV), "Ask and it will be given to you; seek and you will find; knock and the door will be opened to you. For everyone who asks receives; he who seeks finds; and to him who knocks, the door will be opened. Which of you, if his son asks for bread, will give him a stone? Or if he asks for a fish, will give him a snake? If you, then, though you are evil, know how to give good gifts to your children, how much more will your Father in heaven give good gifts to those who ask him!" God is not capricious; rather, God is eager to love and support the children of God. It is the very nature of God and can be no other way. It grieves the Holy Spirit to presume that God is not good. Faith is trusting in the goodness of God and in the providence of God. When we pray in faith, we know that God desires to give us the good gifts when we are ready to receive them. The fruits of the Spirit are love, joy, peace, patience, kindness, goodness, faithfulness, gentleness, and self-control. See Galatians 5:22. These are what we should be asking for in our prayer, and these are the gifts that God wants to give us, and God also wants to give us gifts of the Spirit for the building up of the Body of Christ.

Jesus strictly warns us about making a show of prayer for the sake of winning the approval of others. Our conversations with

God are not for show or profit. Long prayers, loud prayers, eloquent prayers, esoteric prayers, self-aggrandizing prayers, and prayers that pay are explicitly against the will of God. According to Matthew 6:5-8 (NRSV), "And whenever you pray, do not be like the hypocrites; for they love to stand and pray in the synagogues and at the street corners, so that they may be seen by others. Truly I tell you, they have received their reward. But whenever you pray, go into your room and shut the door and pray to your Father who is in secret; and your Father who sees in secret will reward you. When you are praying, do not heap up empty phrases as the Gentiles do; for they think that they will be heard because of their many words. Do not be like them, for your Father knows what you need before you ask him."

Through prayer, we can learn everything we need to know. All the truth that we are capable of understanding will be revealed to us in time. All that was left unsaid or unrecorded in the Gospels can be revealed to us through prayer. Jesus greatly desires to have this ongoing conversation with us. He wants to speak to us and he wants us to listen to him. It is necessary for us to have this time and attentiveness in order for Jesus to have this conversation with us that will transform our lives. In John 16:12-13 (NRSV), "I still have many things to say to you, but you cannot bear them now. When the Spirit of truth comes, he will guide you into all the truth; for he will not speak on his own, but will speak whatever he hears, and he will declare to you the things that are to come."

Do you know that Jesus prays for us and his Apostle John has recorded that prayer? The following is that prayer intact without comment, so that you may know how Jesus prays for you.

In John 17:1-26 (NRSV), "After Jesus had spoken these words, he looked up to heaven and said, 'Father, the hour has come; glorify your Son so that the Son may glorify you, since you have given him authority over all people, to give eternal life to all whom you have given him. And this is eternal life, that they may know you, the only true God, and Jesus Christ whom you have sent. I glorified you on earth by finishing the work that you gave me to do. So now, Father, glorify me in your own presence with the glory that I had in your presence before the world existed. I have made your name known to those whom you gave me from the world. They were yours, and you gave them to me, and they have kept your word. Now they know that everything you have given me is from you; for the words that you gave to me I have given to them, and they have received them and know in truth that I came from you; and they have believed that you sent me. I am asking on their behalf; I am not asking on behalf of the world, but on behalf of those whom you gave me, because they are yours. All mine are yours, and yours are mine; and I have been glorified in them. And now I am no longer in the world, but they are in the world, and I am coming to you. Holy Father, protect them in your name that you have given me, so that they may be one, as we are one. While I was with them, I protected them in your name that you have given me. I guarded them, and not one of them was lost except the one destined to be lost, so that the scripture might be fulfilled. But now I am coming to you, and I speak these things in the world so that they may have my joy made complete in themselves. I have given them your word, and the world has hated them because they do not belong to the world, just as I do not belong to the world. I am not asking you to take them out of the world, but I ask you to protect them from the evil one. They do not belong to the world, just as I do not belong to the world. Sanctify them in the truth; your word is truth. As you have sent me into the world, so I have sent them into the world. And for their sakes I sanctify myself, so that they also may be sanctified in truth. I ask not only on behalf of these, but also on behalf of those who will believe in me through their word, that they may all be one. As you, Father, are in me and I am in you, may they also be in us, so that the world may believe that you have sent me. The glory that you have given me I have given them, so that they may be one, as we are one, I in them and you in me, that they may become completely one, so that the world may know that you have sent me and have loved them even as you have loved me. Father, I desire that those also, whom you have given me, may be with me where I am, to see my glory, which you have given me because you loved me before the foundation of the world. Righteous Father, the world does not know you, but I know you; and these know that you have sent me. I made your name known to them, and I will make it known, so that the love with which you have loved me may be in them, and I in them."

CHAPTER 12

MIRACLES

There are so many miracles recorded in the Gospels and in the rest of the New Testament, it would take a large book to explore them adequately. This will only be a small selection of the miracles in the Gospels and how they reveal the nature of Jesus. There are many more miracles recorded than I chose to list, and there were untold thousands of miracles that are unrecorded in the Bible. There is no reason to doubt these miracles unless one chooses to doubt the divine nature of Jesus. The history of the past two thousand years is filled with countless miracles attributed to Jesus. In recent times, there has been an explosion of miracle stories published. Millions of people are testifying to near death experiences frequently with Jesus appearing to them. One has to be close-minded and hard-hearted to ignore miracles in this modern age.

Healing Miracles
Jesus was best known in his time as a miracle healer. He was frequently mobbed by people in the hope that he would heal them. His fame spread beyond Israel and he was remembered as a faith healer after his death. In the ancient world, the science of medicine and healing was very primitive. Average life expectancy in the

Roman world was around thirty years. Doctors were often more dangerous than helpful, and doctors were prohibitively expensive for the poor which were the overwhelming majority of the population. It is stated in the Gospels that Jesus was frequently met with a frenzied mob seeking healing. It is reported that he healed all who asked him. He healed people who we would classify with mental disorders and he healed people with incurable physical disorders. If one looks carefully at the healing miracles, there is almost always a faith element in the healing. One may conclude that some degree of faith in Jesus was necessary for the healing to occur.

Interestingly, the demonic spirits that Jesus cast out of people knew Jesus and believed he was the Son of God before his disciples came to the same conclusion. The demons feared him and were well justified in fearing him. Today, there are credible people who have a ministry of deliverance for people who have suffered under demonic oppression. These deliverances from the demonic are occurring by the thousands in the United States and around the world daily. Unfortunately, the gulf between the scientific world view and the spiritual world view has not resulted in an acknowledgement of the healing miracles that are happening all around us. There are courageous doctors who are investigating the importance of faith in healing and are open to miraculous healing. It would be exciting for a scientist to do a rigorous study of recovery and healings that included faith and prayer versus those that excluded faith and prayer. Many pastors have been told of miraculous healings, but these are not widely discussed in the church and rarely are talked about to the general public.

Most people that go into the medical profession are both highly intelligent and compassionate. They have been called by God to use their skills to be instruments of God's healing. It is often said they are the hands and hearts of Jesus Christ in the world. Their religious backgrounds and beliefs are not what determines their vocation, although it might. The work that they do is the work of Jesus whether they appreciate it or not. The people in the healing professions are called by God to their vocation. The work being done in hospitals today make miracles routine. Advances in modern medicine will only rapidly increase the miraculous work of the healers. This is God's doing. Of course, our cooperation is vital to the will of God being done on earth as it is in heaven. The wonderful advances in medical science will become far greater when the spiritual dimension is incorporated in the healing profession.

As a patient, we must take responsibility for our healing. The medical people and God cannot help a person who doesn't want to be healed. It is also true that wonderful unexplainable healings can happen with prayer and faith. This is deeper than the mental state of the patient and delves into the spiritual state of the person. For example, if a person believes they are condemned by God, they may not indicate that outwardly, but they have no hope or faith in healing. A person may be suffering chronic pain and appear to be depressed, but they have a strong faith and are expecting healing. Drugs can mask and confuse the state of the mind and of the soul. Patients need to boldly request prayers from the doctors and nurses who attend them. If this is refused by your doctor, you need a different doctor. These prayers do not have to conform to a specific religious formula; they only have to be sincere.

Miracles are an extraordinary event brought about by a supernatural agent. They can heal the sick and they can meet an immediate need. They can bring the dead back to life. All of these extraordinary events are ultimately transitory. The sick will eventually become unwell and die. Their immediate needs will be satisfied for a time and then the inevitable will reappear. Even the raising of the dead is transitory. So what is the underlying purpose of miracles? The purpose of miracles is faith. Miracles happen in the conditions of faith and build faith. Faith is not transitory because it has eternal consequences. Our purpose in this life is to love God completely and to love our neighbor as ourselves. Faith takes us on the right course. Airplanes rely on a guidance system to constantly adjust their course to achieve arriving at their destination. We need constant course corrections to arrive at our destination. Miracles happen when we have been blown off course.

The following are a representative sample of Jesus healing physical diseases and disabilities: Luke 5:12-16, cleansing of the leper; Luke 6:6-11, Jesus heals the man with the withered hand; Luke 7:1-10, healing the Centurion's slave; Luke 5:17-26, healing of paralyzed man; Luke 8:1-3, Jesus heals Mary Magdalene; Luke 13:10-17, healing of crippled woman; Luke 14:1-16, healing man with dropsy; Luke 17:11-19, healing of ten lepers; and John 5:2-47, healing at the pool of Bethesda.

Jesus and the demonic

Mental illness is as old as human history and has been perplexing up until the most recent times. Recently, we have discovered the use of chemicals to modify brain chemistry to alter behavior. This has been successful some of the time and failed some of the time. Unfortunately, many people have committed suicide while taking properly prescribed medications. Psychoactive drugs are still in their infancy and promise better results in the future. Globally, mental illness was understood to be a spiritual problem and was treated accordingly. The scientific mindset has dismissed this spiritual understanding as nonsense. Thousands of people have been restored to well-being by prayer and this is ancient global fact. When the mental health profession opens their minds to the traditions of the importance of prayer, they will have the tools for effectively restoring people to a beautiful life. Science and faith are not mutually exclusive or at odds with each other. They need to be seen as collaborators in this complex world.

Jesus casting out of demonic spirits is not magic. Jesus was practicing an ancient healing art that is still in use today. Jesus was especially effective in this art because he was the source of this art form. His ability to deliver people from demonic oppression was to restore people into a healthy relationship with God and with their community. The underlying goal was to create faith in a loving God.

The following are a representative sample of Jesus delivering people from demonic spirits: Matthew 9:23-26, Mark 1:23-28, Jesus heals a demoniac; Mark 2:1-12, Mark 1:40-45, Mark 1:29-31, Luke 4:40-41, Jesus heals multitudes; Mark 5:1-20, Jesus heals the demoniac; Mark 5:21-43, Jesus heals women; Mark 6, healing many at Gennesaret; Mark 7:31-37, healing of a deaf man; Mark 9:14-29, healing of a boy possessed; and Mark 10:46-52, healing of blind man on road to Jericho.

Miracles of Nature

Miracles are also referred to as signs in the Gospel of John. This gives us a clearer understanding of miracles as signs for us to deepen our faith. Jesus came into this world to change the human heart. He did not come to change the nature of our world. He did not eliminate disease but he has shown us how to conquer disease. He did not come to eliminate hunger but he has shown us how to share our resources. This world is full of beauty and abundance, and it is full of dangers and disasters. Jesus did these miracles to encourage our faith in him as the Son of God. These miracles were done before many witnesses and were recorded within the lifetime of many of the persons who witnessed these miracles. Even his enemies did not deny his miracles. They accused him of being in league with the devil which gave him the power to do these things. His disciples witnessed these miracles and were convinced Jesus was exactly the Messiah he claimed to be. In the New Testament, we have four historical documents and several letters, all written within a few decades of the events described. The living witnesses to these events became many of the early followers of the movement. They would not have risked their lives for a fraud. The proof of the reliability of Jesus' miracles are the historical writings in the New Testament, the rapid growth and expansion of the earliest Christian communities, the passion and self-sacrifice of the apostles, and the ongoing miracles and faith of the early church. All of this took place in the life span of the first witnesses of the miracles in a world that was hostile and often murderous toward believers in Jesus Christ. It was extremely dangerous to profess Jesus as Savior, and the believers not only prevailed but they triumphed. That is the most extraordinary miracle of the history of humankind. The truth of Jesus Christ flourished against the vigorous persecution of the Roman Empire, the most powerful empire the world has ever known. This can only be described as a miracle. It happened because Jesus is what he told us he is, and he lives.

Some of the miracles Jesus performed are in Matthew 14:20-33, Jesus walks on water; Luke 5:1-11, miraculous catch of fish; Mark 4:35-41, stilling the storm; Mark 8:1-10, Jesus feeds four thousand; and John 6:1-15, Jesus feeds five thousand.

Miracles of Resurrection

Bringing a person back to life from death is a miracle of the greatest significance. The greatest fear of humanity is the fear of death. This fear drives people into many false pursuits. The popular saying, "The one who dies with the most toys wins," is totally absurd, but not false for many of us in a materialistic culture. What did the person win? They are valued and judged by their possessions by whom? Other materialists may see life solely as a competition to see who can acquire the most stuff, but we can only hope most people are wiser than that superficial world view. How a person loved others and what they contributed to society are surely infinitely more important to how we esteem a person's life. There are many saintly people who have enriched the world with their love and charitable works like Mother Theresa or Saint Francis, and they died without any possessions. How many contemporary billionaires will be long remembered after their deaths? There are numerous examples of tyrants with enormous power over people for a period of time who may be remembered for their cruelty and the misery they created in the world, and we are glad they are gone. Life is typically a few decades of an opportunity to make the best of this opportunity we have been given as social beings. In this world that God created, there is a design and a purpose for each of us to achieve with the little life we have been given. One life is completely sufficient for us to realize who we are and do our best to realize our potential. The goal has been simply stated as, "The purpose of life is to glorify God." We glorify God by following Jesus and obeying the commandments. This is not hard to understand. With the help of God, it is also something we can do with the abilities and circumstances we find in our life. There are many saints alive in this world that are little known, living the way God created us to live.

Resurrection has become almost routine events in the modern medical setting. People are brought back from death where CPR and other resuscitation techniques are available. The reality is these measures may give us added years of life, but we will all die and not come back ever. When Jesus brought back from death to life the boy, the little girl, and Lazarus, they lived and died and we know nothing further about them. When Jesus died and came back to life, he never died again and he lives amongst us. This is the resurrection to eternal life that is the paramount message of the Gospels, and hopefully our certain future as well.

In a time of crisis, we may call out to Jesus to save us from death and say a prayer that is answered. We may die and be resuscitated. We may prolong our life by months or years, but this is all fleeting. We have nothing to fear from death if we know where we are going after we leave this world. If there is no god and there is no life after death, then nothing has any meaning so it doesn't make any difference whether we live or die. The atheist should be as indifferent to death as they are to God and eternal salvation. To the atheist, existence is of absolutely no consequence. If a person has a suspicion there might be a Supreme Being, it would make sense to investigate what wise people have taught on this topic since death is inevitable. There are possible outcomes from this life that could be exceedingly rewarding or horrible. It is irrational to ignore the possible outcomes based on the wisdom of thousands of years. What if it is true that when our body perishes our soul lives on? There are billions of people living today who believe this to be true.

Christians believe that Jesus is the first born from the dead and he will raise up to heaven those who believe in him. That is the deeper understanding of the miracle of the resurrection of Jesus. For example, in Matthew 9:23-26, Jesus raises a little girl; Luke 7:11-17, raising the widow's son from death; John 11:1-44, raising of Lazarus. Detailed descriptions of the resurrection of Jesus can be found in the following books: Matthew Chapter 28, Mark Chapter 16, Luke Chapter 24, and John Chapters 20-21

Near Death Experiences
The miracle of resurrection is happening at an amazing rate in our modern world. They are called near death experiences. It is estimated that one out of twenty Americans has had a near death experience. Out of a population of over three hundred million, that equates to sixty million people have had some form of NDE. This phenomenon is global and there are examples throughout history going back thousands of years. There are hundreds of these testimonies on websites such as the International Association for Near Death Studies (IANDS), Near Death Experience Research Foundation (NDERF), and NewHeavenNewEarth (NHNE). God is speaking directly to the world to wake up before it is too late. The criticism of these experiences states they are anecdotal so they cannot be proven scientifically. Millions of people testify to remarkably similar experiences, and some skeptics dismiss these testimonies as irrelevant. If many people sincerely warned you that

a certain snake had a venomous bite, would you ignore their warning? Do you have to be bitten by that snake to decide if it was toxic or not? Jesus gave us the map of the universe with his life, and it is clearly defined what our life and death is about. He offers this in love and asks only for that love to be reciprocated. What he did he will do for us if we trust him. The ultimate miracle is offered to us that will make everything known to us, and raise us up to be more glorious than we can imagine in our heavenly home.

CHAPTER 13

CALLED

God is calling you and me. Jesus said, "For many are called, but few are chosen," Matthew 22:14 (NRSV). You are called. We will discuss whether you are chosen later in this chapter. We begin our discussion of the call by clarifying what we mean by the call. This has several levels of meaning in the spiritual understanding.

God is mysterious, and God has revealed the true nature of God to us in numerous ways. So we know God by God's self-revelation. This revelation comes to us in Holy Scriptures, traditions, creation, reason, and experience. The call comes to us on all these levels. The call is to know, love, and serve God. How we do that is specific to each individual. Sit at a busy airport or train station and watch the people go by. They all have a common physiology, but they are remarkably different in every way. If you were to stop them and interview them, you would be overwhelmed at how different they are from each other in background, thoughts, and character. If you tried to interview people, how many would be willing to respond? For a variety of reasons, many would refuse to be interviewed. Possibly the majority of people would not even stop to consider the proposition. Most people are too busy to be interviewed. How many people take the time to seriously consider their relationship with God? God does not impose upon us, nor does God demand our attention. Too many people only think of God during a crisis. God's call is too often ignored. The Scriptures tell us God is omniscient and knows us each as unique individuals. Every one of us wonderfully made persons are known and loved by God. This may be too amazing to comprehend, yet it is true. The call and response is unique with every individual. Our response to God covers the whole range of possibilities. To be chosen is how we respond to the call.

Since God created us, it is appropriate to think of God as our parent. Jesus frequently referred to God as Daddy (Abba in Aramaic), and Jesus made references to God as Mother also. God is something like our Father, Mother, Brother, Sister, and Friend. God is comparable to family relations or any close relation. God is like our grandfather, grandmother, aunt, or uncle. God can be compared to these because we use these as representative of God's love for us as we have experienced love in this life. God is also named the good shepherd, living water, mighty mountain, and the bread of life, etc. In family relationships, one expects communication. The cruelest action a family member can do to sever the family is to break communicating with another member of the family. Unfortunately, most if not all families have had this happen at one time or another. This is an action of very real domestic violence done to the family. Does a mother or father stop loving the child who abandons the family? It is impossible that they are capable of not loving their child. They are hurt, they are angry, they try to deal with the pain, and they attempt to live beyond the grief. How many times do they think to themselves, "If only they would call?" God, who is more loving than a human, calls us.

We are not orphans in this world. We have our biological family and we have our heavenly Creator. God calls to us all the time through the Scriptures, creation, reason, traditions, and experiences. God also calls to us through the witness of other people and by instances of the Holy Spirit. God desires a relationship with us. God really likes us because we are God's children. We may be naughty children but we are still loved. In some instances, God admires a little weirdness and wildness in the family. Many characters in the Bible who are called by God exhibit unconventional behavior. If God is calling all the children all the time over the entire world, why is there such disconnect between the Creator and the children? Using the analogy of family, how can one have a relationship with God when one does know who their parent is? To connect with God, one must have some basic belief in God. False gods, also known as idols, are a serious obstacle to connecting with God. Idols can be egotism, lust, power, control, materialism, and anything we worship that is not God. Idolatry is a diversion away from God.

Idolatry in the broadest application of the word can even take the form of idolatry of religious traditions. For many people, there is reluctance to even entertain the concept of God. Hidden in many subconscious minds are aversions to God because of trauma associated with religious experiences. The most successful addiction treatment programs use the term Higher Power because they appreciate that the very word God is intimidating to many people. God who knows everything is very tolerant of terminology because God judges by the heart and not appearances. When an addict calls upon their Higher Power, God is paying attention and ready to respond. This cry of the sinner is the response God has been calling and calling for a very long time. God is patiently waiting by the phone for the ring. Before that person called to God, God was calling to that person.

This call is expressed as personal through Jesus. The lyrics to an old hymn by Will L. Thompson tell us something about God's call: "Softly and tenderly Jesus is calling, calling for you and for me; see, on the portals He's waiting and watching, watching for you and for me. Come home, come home; ye who are weary come home; earnestly, tenderly, Jesus is calling, calling, 'O sinner, come home!'"

The Gospels show us Jesus, making it vividly clear that the call is personal. Jesus calls his disciples by name. See Matthew 4:18-22, Mark 1:16-20, Luke 5:2-11, and John 1:35-42. We will never know whether there was any relationship between Jesus and the men he called prior to his calling them to follow him. The call to follow seems to be an almost supernatural compulsion to obey. It is obvious from the Gospels that the disciples did not understand who Jesus was when they chose to follow him. Jesus was a thirty-year-old itinerant rabbi with no credentials. He must have had a powerful charisma to attract people the way he called them and they followed. The Bible tells us that he called them by name. Did he know these men, or was this a supernatural knowing which would imply he knew more about them than just their name? Paul had a direct call by the resurrected Jesus on the road to Damascus. Millions of women and men have experienced such a call on them to follow Jesus in the past two thousand years. It is possible to refuse such a call but the typical response is to follow and obey. The charisma of Jesus is as real today as it was when he called his disciples. If the door is closed to Jesus, the one locked inside will never know him. When he knocks, the door must be opened.

The examples in the Gospels are all a call to discipleship and ministry. This is the traditional understanding of a call, but there are other ways to receive a call. The word "vocation" means a call to a type of work. It is common to refer to professions as vocations such as doctors and lawyers. Are not some called to nursing, teaching, social work, administration, and childrearing? Farming is a vocation, musician, business, machinist, and so on for every work conceivable. The vocation of marriage may be the highest calling of all. Every type of work is suitable to be a vocation, but not everyone employed in that work was necessarily called to that work. There are men and women in ministry who do not belong in those fields. This is true for all situations. It is a struggle for some to identify what their calling is in life. Does God call people into their life work? This is what is suggested by the Scriptures. We even learn that all work is for God's purposes for those who love God in Romans 8:28. The beauty of a free society is that people have the opportunity to pursue their call and to excel in it.

How do we appreciate that the call to marriage may be the greatest call in life? The call to raise a family is the foundational call for humankind. When Jesus said, "Many are called but few are chosen," what specific call was he referring to? This saying is at the conclusion of the parable of the kingdom of heaven being like a wedding party in Matthew 22:1-14. A guest did not come prepared for the wedding and was apparently not invited. So he was ejected. This teaches us that we should respond to our calling and not go where we have not been invited. In this parable, many people were invited who did not respond. So this is applicable to the call today where many are called to a specific vocation but do not respond, and those who are not called should not attend.

Real happiness in life is knowing one's call and being able to pursue it. A prescription for misery is to enter into the vocation that is not suitable for the individual. This is where reason, experience, and tradition are important parts of the call process. It is a joyous and important responsibility to help a person identify their call and discover the ways to achieve it.

The whole creation calls us to God. The spectacle of beauty in nature when studied creates awe. From the micro to the macro, it is all too wonderful to behold. It is hard to understand how a person cannot consider that there is a Designer behind the design. The discipline of science only unveils greater complexity and wonder in the creation. The Grand Canyon has brought people to an appreciation of a Creator. The amazing complexity of DNA brings us to a deeper appreciation of the Creative genius in our world. The vast universe with trillions of galaxies, each containing billions of stars and countless planets just being discovered, affirm the certainty there is an Intelligence that has created this. The laws of physics of the universe existed before the Big Bang began. How wonderful to consider God shaping, creating, and unfolding the creation. Every sunrise and sunset glows with the glory of God. The whole creation calls us to reverence for to the Supreme Being. Our reverence for the creation is a call to be good stewards of the world. This was the first call given to humans.

The church is a body of people called together, which is precisely what the original word "ecclesia" meant in Greek. The church building is not the church. The church is a mix of people drawn from the world. Is everyone called into the church? It is difficult imagining who Jesus would exclude from the church since he deliberately chose all kinds of sinners for his companions. There are not many churches today that have the same kind of diversity as those called to Jesus when he was ministering. Most churches resemble clubs for people seeking others of similar racial, economic, and cultural status. The church is enriched when it develops a heterogeneous congregation rather than homogenous congregation. The church is not called to think tribal but universal. The church that follows Jesus would aspire to be inclusive and not exclusive. The church is in constant need of reform to be faithful to its call. Followers of Jesus are called to be a part of the church, and not to live in isolation. The church is where the called are obedient to God in the community of the faithful.

Spiritual discernment is essential to knowing and following our call. Discernment is one of the most important lessons in the human experience. There is a difference between wisdom and knowledge. Spiritual discernment is the fruit of wisdom which comes from knowledge. One cannot know the call in our lives without spiritual discernment. Fortunately, we are not alone in acquiring the ability to discern. We have access to wise and Christ-centered people to guide us and instruct us on our journey of discovery. When we explore our vocation, we must seek wise elders who have already walked the path we are considering. We have the guidance of the Scriptures that contain the accumulated wisdom of inspired testimonies to show us the way through the plains and mountains on our adventure. Perhaps most importantly, we have access to God by the indwelling Spirit of God to pray to and to listen to whenever we need direction. Between the wisdom of mentors, scriptural example, and the Holy Spirit, we are inevitably going to find our bearings on the journey. To pursue a call without serious attention to the discipline of seeking guidance from the sources mentioned is foolhardy and can lead to disaster. God calls us to be successful in life. Jesus tells us in John 15:11 (NRSV), "I have said these things to you so that my joy may be in you, and that your joy may be complete." God did not make us to be failures in this world. God made us to be filled with joy in life well lived by realizing our call.

We are called to eternal life in this life. This is known as realized eschatology. It is much like the term being saved or being born again. When we stop relying solely upon ourselves and running our lives constrained by the limitations of our ego, and we make God the driving force of our lives, our whole perspective changes. Life is radically different. We gain an understanding of things that previously had been unsolvable puzzles. We appreciate that which we despised before, and our hearts are filled with love. We know that we know that we know. Our lives based on a solid foundation flourish in this world and we no longer flounder through life. We came from heaven and we are created to return to heaven. Heaven is not alien territory; it becomes our home. We know we will arrive at the destination that is our true home after this adventure in this world is over. Our call is serious business.

CHAPTER 14

DISCIPLESHIP

A disciple of Jesus Christ is a person who follows him in thought, word, and deed. When a person makes the decision to become a follower of Jesus, they have set a course that is counter to the ways of the world. The way of Jesus Christ is often in conflict with the culture, which creates difficulties for the disciple. Discipleship is not easy, the rewards are not immediate, and sacrifice is mandatory. "He called the crowd with his disciples, and said to them, 'If any want to become my followers, let them deny themselves and take up their cross and follow me,'" Mark 8:34 (NRSV). Discipleship is a process that requires a lifetime of complete dedication. It is not a sprint race; rather, it is a long distance race. The Christian Testaments are overflowing with teachings and suggestions for the disciple. The Gospels contain many frank and revealing situations that a disciple will face. Jesus continually seeks disciples, and challenges those who respond to his call with ever more complex levels of difficulty. Life without Jesus is simpler, but so much less rewarding that the absence of Jesus is not an option.

To receive the salvation of Jesus is the first step in the arduous spiritual journey of the disciple of Jesus. God's will is for all people to be saved through faith in Jesus Christ.

In 1 Timothy 2:1-4 (NRSV), we read, "First of all, then, I urge that supplications, prayers, intercessions, and thanksgivings be made for everyone, for kings and all who are in high positions, so that we may lead a quiet and peaceable life in all godliness and dignity. This is right and is acceptable in the sight of God our Savior, who desires everyone to be saved and to come to the knowledge of the truth." The disciples of Jesus Christ are required to propagate the faith in peace with all people. In Christianity, there cannot be coerced conversions. Before we try to convert people to Christ, we have to convert ourselves. The process of discipleship begins with self-examination.

We need to begin the journey of following Christ with a thorough examination of ourselves, which is a painful process. The human being is a master of self-deception, and the deeper we go into our shadows and secrets, the more we will evade the truth of who we are. The nature of our shadow side is denial and deceit. We must earnestly pray for the guidance of the Holy Spirit and for the courage to discover the truth. Even though we may despise what we find, there is comfort in the fact that Jesus chose us first and we only responded to him. "For those whom he foreknew he also predestined to be conformed to the image of his Son, in order that he might be the firstborn within a large family. And those whom he predestined he also called; and those whom he called he also justified; and those whom he justified he also glorified. What then are we to say about these things? If God is for us, who is against us?" Romans 8:29-31 (NRSV). God has called us to be his disciples, and those he called also the justified. In spite of the many flaws and weaknesses that we discover deep in ourselves, we are the chosen instrument of God's will. As imperfect as this instrument may be, it is the perfect device in God's plan for the salvation of the world. Who are we to deny what God has chosen? It is irrelevant how weak we may be, because given the opportune time, we will have the strength of the Spirit of Christ to accomplish God's will.

With God as our ally, what do we have to fear? We certainly cannot allow our own self-doubt and deprecations to be our saboteur. Discipleship is living the faith, trusting in the power of God, and striving to serve Christ. The awesome truth is God loves us. We are the chosen children of God.

Discipleship is putting our faith into action. It is one thing to say that we believe Jesus Christ is Lord and Savior, and it is quite another to put that faith into the crucible of transforming ourselves and interacting with the world. To follow Christ, we must know him.

There are three ways that we can know Jesus, and they are the Bible, prayer, and the church. Firstly, we learn about Jesus by studying the scriptures, and most especially the four Gospels. The more one reads and meditates on the life and teachings of Jesus, the more real he becomes. There is no substitute for knowing Jesus by reading the Gospels and the rest of the Bible. This needs to be a daily part of your life if you are interested in truly knowing him and following him. You need to put yourself in the Gospels and imagine the events from the different perspectives of the individuals. You need to become the leper that was healed, the blind man that was given sight, the prodigal son, the Pharisees, the crowds who wanted him crucified, the woman who was caught in adultery, the Roman soldier who nailed him to the cross, Mary Magdalene meeting the resurrected Christ at the tomb, Peter who denied him three times, and Jesus himself looking down from the cross saying, "Father, forgive them; for they do not know what they are doing," Luke 23:34 (NRSV). Become all of these people, and identify with them, because there is a part of each of them in each of us. The purpose for studying the scriptures is to incorporate them into your being. There is the Spirit of God in the scriptures; let this Spirit of Christ become your Spirit. The only way to receive the inspired word of God as in the Scriptures is to read the Bible prayerfully. Slowly read and reread over and over. Ask God to speak to you from the Word of God. God will speak to your heart and mind in the still small voice of God. You will come to know it because it is the Holy Spirit that lives in you.

Secondly, we come to know Christ through prayer. Prayer is growing in intimacy with the God through conversation. Prayer is not simply trying to tell God what to do, or what you want. Prayer is consciously speaking to God in the most honest manner possible and allowing God to speak to us. God wants to have this conversation with us. "Likewise the Spirit helps us in our weakness; for we do not know how to pray as we ought, but that very Spirit intercedes with sighs too deep for words," Romans 8:26 (NRSV). The purpose of prayer is to change who? We are the ones who are to be changed by prayer. Prayer is allowing the Spirit of God to speak to us and for us to be conformed in our hearts and minds to God. Since God already knows everything about you, it is only sensible to be really honest with God. Tell God everything you think and feel. Beg for help. Confess your sins and give them up to God. God is the best teacher you will ever know. God is patient, kind, and forgiving.

Thirdly, we learn from the church which was created by the Holy Spirit to bring us to Jesus. We gather to be the Body of Christ where he is the sole head. Christianity is relational. Christianity exists in community. There is a common misconception that being a Christian is all about the welfare of the individual. This is not Christian. Jesus Christ was completely about his relationship with God, and his relationship with people living in community. The followers of Jesus Christ exist in community, and they do not exist as isolated entities. If a person has the Spirit of Jesus Christ, this Spirit will compel them to seek and be part of the community of faith. There is a terrible deception in contemporary society that claims you can be a Christian without being part of the Body of Christ. This is completely untrue. If one reads one Corinthians Chapters 12 and 13, you will find that a Christian is part of the Body of Christ. Each individual is given gifts for the building up of the Body.

Being a part of the community of the church is messy business, because all human beings are flawed sinners and come with their own agendas, both obvious and hidden. Following Jesus Christ is working with our brothers and sisters to grow spiritually in the way, truth, and life of Christ. When Jesus calls us into salvation, he is calling us into the church. "My sheep hear my voice. I know them, and they follow me," John 10:27 (NRSV). We are in his fold, the church. We are called into the church to build up the Body of Christ. The Body of Christ is as essential to the individual Christian as the individual is essential to the church.

Many people go to church to be entertained, and they move from church to church looking for better entertainment. The church of Jesus Christ does not need to be in the entertainment business. The church exists to be the Body of Christ which worships and serves God. Worship is the work of praising God, and is not necessarily about pleasing ourselves. The pleasure in worship is to please God. Serving God is the work of mission and evangelism, and is not necessarily about amusing ourselves. In today's society, many people have abandoned the church. We have become spectators who expect to be amused. Frequently, this has become a vicious cycle of people seeking to gratify their self-interest, neglecting the call to discipleship, and the church becomes increasingly irrelevant to the commandment of Christ to do mission and evangelism. The church is ever in need of reform. It is up to the individual members of the church to make that reform happen. This is what Jesus asked us to do when he calls us to be his followers.

One of the clearest commandments of Jesus is called the Great Commission. In Matthew 28:18-20 (NRSV), we read, "And Jesus came and said to them, 'All authority in heaven and on earth has been given to me. Go therefore and make disciples of all nations, baptizing them in the name of the Father and of the Son and of the Holy Spirit, and teaching them to obey everything that I have commanded you. And remember, I am with you always, to the end of the age.'" The disciples of Jesus Christ are people sent out into the world. The world may be family, the immediate neighborhood, the city, the country, the region, the nation, or the world. The operative word in the great commission is "go." As followers of Jesus Christ, we are to go out into the world doing the work of Jesus Christ. Make disciples, baptize them, and teach them; this is what Jesus commands us to do. This commandant is not only for a few elite professionals; rather, this commandment is for all Christians. There are many different gifts of the Spirit for the building up of the Body of Christ. Each person may be given one or a few gifts. Not all people are gifted by the Spirit to be evangelists, but all people who are part of the Body of Christ are gifted by the Spirit to contribute to evangelism in some form. Their gift may be in hospitality, administration, or financial support; these are all critical parts of successful evangelism. Not all people are gifted as missionaries but every member of the Body of Christ is responsible for the support and work of the missions of the church. Just as each member of the church contributes to the work of worship, so does each member of the church have an equally important share in contributing to the mission and evangelism of the church.

The call to follow Jesus Christ comes with a warning that we are called to make sacrifices. This has been called the cost of discipleship in Luke 9:23-26 (NRSV), "Then he said to them all, 'If any want to become my followers, let them deny themselves and take up their cross daily and follow me. For those who want to save their life will lose it, and those who lose their life for my sake will save it. What does it profit them if they gain the whole world, but lose or forfeit themselves? Those who are ashamed of me and of my words, of them the Son of Man will be ashamed when he comes in his glory and the glory of the Father and of the holy angels.'" To follow Jesus Christ is not all fun and games. To take up one's cross and follow Jesus will cost us to some degree money, time, popularity, worldly success, self-contentment, and control of our lives. The cross is the symbol of sacrifice, and if we take up the cross to follow Jesus, then we are to sacrifice daily. "If you wish to be perfect, go, sell your possessions, and give the money to the poor, and you will have treasure in heaven; then come, follow me," Matthew 19:21 (NRSV). This is the cost of discipleship and very few of us are willing to make the sacrifice. But it is better to do this gradually, than not do it at all. Each of us grows at our own rate according to our ability and understanding. We do not become saints overnight; it is a lifetime process. The good news is that Jesus is with us every step of the way. He is especially present when we are together in community of faith.

Discipleship is becoming a member of and contributing to the Body of Christ. Saint Paul states it succinctly, "Now you are the body of Christ and individually members of it," 1 Corinthians 12:27 (NRSV). In Chapters 12 and 13 of his first letter to the Corinthians, he explains the important role that each member has in relationship to one another. This is how the Spirit of Christ has designed the church to be the incarnation of Jesus Christ in this world. Jesus is the sole head, and he leads us by his Spirit which he has given to each of his followers. Every disciple has their role in building up the Body of Christ that was given to them by Jesus. "The gifts he gave were that some would be apostles, some prophets, some evangelists, some pastors and teachers, to equip the saints for the work of ministry, for building up the body of Christ, until all of us come to the unity of the faith and of the knowledge of the Son of God, to maturity, to the measure of the full stature of Christ," Ephesians 4:11-13 (NRSV). Through the church, we become mature Christians so that we may know the fullness of Jesus Christ. If you want to know Jesus, you can know him completely by being part of his body. Although there is sacrifice involved in carrying the cross, the reward of knowing Jesus far exceeds what little sacrifices we make. This may be impossible to explain, but it is part of the journey of faith that Jesus leads us on. If you ask a mature

Christian whether it was worth it or not, you will find that the joy and rewards of knowing Jesus surpass any other sacrifices that we were called to make.

Jesus gives each of his beloved followers gifts of the Spirit for the building up of the church. Most people are given one gift, and some are given a few gifts. No one is given all of the gifts. In the scriptures, more than 26 gifts can be identified. It is the obligation of every Christian to know and use their gifts for the building up of the church. "Now there are varieties of gifts, but the same Spirit; and there are varieties of services, but the same Lord; and there are varieties of activities, but it is the same God who activates all of them in everyone. To each is given the manifestation of the Spirit for the common good," 1 Corinthians 12:4-7 (NRSV). These gifts that are given are not in competition with each other or for the inflation of an individual's ego. The gifts of the Spirit are given to work in harmony with each other under the leadership of Jesus. His leadership is readily identified by the quality of his love which is the supreme gift of all. In the conclusion of St. Paul's description of the gifts of the Spirit, we read Chapter 13 of his first letter to the Corinthians, often called the love chapter. The love chapter is introduced with the concluding sentence of Chapter 12:31 (NRSV): "But strive for the greater gifts. And I will show you a still more excellent way." The most excellent way is the way of Christ love, and it is beautifully described in Chapter 13. This is the way of Jesus and of his followers.

Discipleship is never easy, but it is the very reason why we were created. To know God, to love God, and to do God's will is to follow the way of Christ. The grace that we have been given is his real presence to loveus and guide us in every step of the journey in this world and in the next. "And remember, I am with you always, to the end of the age," Matthew 28:20 (NRSV). We are not alone because we have Jesus, the Holy Spirit, and our brothers and sisters in Christ to love and support us and on our journey.

One of the most perfect joys in life is to belong and be obedient to an organic vital community where we can give and receive love. The vitality of the community depends on a balance of adherence to shared beliefs and values with the ability to be creative and redefine conventions. Imbalance between rigidity and chaos can be disturbing enough to destroy the cohesiveness of the community. Conflicts are inevitable and should be used as opportunities for growth and maturity. With Jesus as the head of the church, disciples will thrive and be enabled to glorify God. The church is an organic congregation of sinners becoming saints. What a joy and privilege to be part of God's garden.

CHAPTER 15
JUDGMENT

The topic of judgment is a threatening subject because we are well aware that we are flawed beings. Christians believe we are all sinners and are saved by grace. All Christians battle with their old nature against their Christ nature. Paul writes so succinctly about this in Romans 7:14-20. We all are painfully reminded daily that sin dwells within us, even though we are devoted to Jesus Christ. We fight the good fight and stand firm in our faith and the conflict continues. Our faith informs us we are assured of our salvation through Jesus' atonement, but how can he really love us that much? This is where faith has to have the dominant power in our hearts and minds. Our faith is not in our worthiness. Christians have been justified and saved by their faith. Our faith is in Jesus, not in ourselves, and he is worthy. Christians need have no anxiety about judgment because of the salvific work of Jesus.

If a person is not a Christian, then they must develop their own plan for going to heaven or whatever they hope is their destiny after this life. In reincarnation, a person's karmic debt determines the conditions of their next life. Will a million times a million lives erase their karmic debt? Christians do not subscribe to reincarnation because they believe that Jesus Christ died for their sins, and they are no longer condemned by their sins; rather, they are made justified by Jesus' sacrifice on the cross and his forgiveness. Some religions have a plan of works righteousness. Christians do believe in righteous works, but not in their efficacy for salvation. Atheists don't think about life after death because to them it is all fairy tales. Judgment is meaningless to atheists because they invent their own moral standards, which presumably are favorable to their conduct. Judgment is a matter of concern to every Christian no matter how strong their faith.

Judgment might be a simple issue for Christians if they believe they are saved. Christians may still question their salvation and only hope they are worthy of heaven. Both Protestants and Catholics believe we are saved and justified by God's grace through faith in Jesus Christ. The role of Jesus Christ in the Christian understanding of judgment is the subject of this chapter. Salvation is the subject covered in chapter seventeen.

The beginning of our understanding of judgment is why does God judge us? Is God a God who is "love and wrath," or is God just love? If God makes no distinction between good and evil, right and wrong, and love and hate, then God is a huge disappointment. Without God's judgment, there is no justice and we live in a universe of absolute chaos. Everything is neither good nor bad; it is just what it is. There is no morality and there is no law. This world of absolute chaos and absence of morality would be hell. In fact, that is exactly what hell is, absolute chaos and absence of morality. In the Bible, the origin of the universe is God creating order from chaos. The biblical theme of God calling us to seek order out of the chaos of our lives is the constant throughout the Scriptures. Justice creates order and prescribes ways of deterring chaos. The reason for having a justice system is to encourage behavior that is healthy and not destructive. The term "God's wrath" is equivalent to the concept of justice. The aim of justice is not punishment; rather, it is to support abundant life. Punishment is a byproduct of chaos and the inevitable consequence of opposition to a just universe. Our legal system's purpose is to define the laws, which are the boundaries of acceptable behavior. It also has specific remedies for violations of the law. The punishments prescribed by the law are the remedy for law breakers. Their purpose is to motivate people to keep the laws. A justice system must have consequences or it is meaningless.

God judges the heart and not by appearances. Humans judge by appearances and we are incapable of knowing another's heart. The justice systems of the world are all flawed because we don't know what God knows about the human heart and we never will. God's justice is perfect because God knows the core of our being. The human justice system seeks to discover the truth of a situation. It is imperfect and is known to make mistakes. There is no argument before God because God knows the truth and God is absolutely fair in God's judgment. In the light of God, truth is absolute. God allows the individual to suffer the consequences of their actions. Their "punishment" is to receive what they have desired. The torment of hell is self-created and not imposed. In the timelessness of Hell, a moment is everlasting.

In the Holiness of God, there is no hint of a shadow of sin. This would be condemnation of all persons, because we are all guilty of sin. Everyone is completely dependent upon the mercy of God. The holiness of God is so opposite of human nature they could not be more different. Humans stand no chance of justifying themselves before a Holy God. Thank God for Jesus. It is Jesus who justifies us. The suffering and death of Jesus is the turning point in human history and our salvation.

The judgment is created into a new concept because our sin is covered by Jesus' sacrifice. We stand justified before a Holy God. The guilty is proclaimed innocent. In Hebrews 4:14-16 (NRSV), we read, "Since, then, we have a great high priest who has passed through the heavens, Jesus, the Son of God, let us hold fast to our confession. For we do not have a high priest who is unable to sympathize with our weaknesses, but we have one who in every respect has been tested as we are, yet without sin. Let us therefore approach the throne of grace with boldness, so that we may receive mercy and find grace to help in time of need." This is the promise of Christian faith. We are judged by God and we are welcomed into heaven by The Holy One because of Jesus our Savior. This is what being saved means. We are rescued, like a drowning person rescued from the crashing waves.

When we believe, trust, follow, and put our faith in Jesus, we are going to heaven. As Paul tells us in Romans 8:38-39 (NRSV), "For I am convinced that neither death, nor life, nor angels, nor rulers, nor things present, nor things to come, nor powers, nor height, nor depth, nor anything else in all creation, will be able to separate us from the love of God in Christ Jesus our Lord." This assurance of the absolute hope of salvation by our faith in Jesus Christ is the core of the Christian faith. When a person puts their life in this hope, everything changes. There is no longer a fear of death, which is the greatest fear that all people suffer. The triumph of God's will over evil is no longer in doubt both for the individual and for the world. Every day becomes possible to live a new life in the promise of living a life pleasing to God. We are no longer slaves to the power of sin and death. We are free to live fully with a peace that surpasses all understanding. The new life we find in our salvation opens our hearts to compassion for all people, even at the expense of our own gains. We eagerly seek our sanctification, which is the very reason we were created from the beginning of time. The enthusiasm for salvation drives us to want all people to experience this new life. The Gospel of Jesus Christ is the "Good News" for the world.

How are people judged who have deliberately rejected Jesus? Their fate is in the hands of a God of justice. Since they have knowingly rejected the salvation offered to them, they stand as sinners on their own. It is hard to imagine what they expected. Does God overlook what they want God to ignore? Since God knows their heart, it is reasonable to believe that God gives them precisely what they desire. They go away from God, away from Jesus, and away from the Saints in heaven. Where they go, they are free to exist, and relish the ways they craved in life. The place they go to is described by Jesus is the outer darkness, which goes by many names. It has been called the underworld, the pit, the void, the abyss, Hades, Sheol, Gehenna, hell, and other names. There has been much speculation about what that place is like and they all fail to convey its real content. Those who find themselves there are devoid of the good things of the world. They are without hope because they refused the hope God offered them in Jesus. They cling to what they believed in this world, which does nothing to gratify their desires. Their souls are in torment because they are without hope or love. God gave them what their hearts desired. Separation from God is hell. God grieves for these lost souls who have rejected God.

People who are ignorant of Jesus are not without hope if they have followed Jesus' teaching in spite of being without Christian understanding. The Spirit of Christ made the world and has been active in the entire world from the beginning of creation. People who have never been touched by Christianity have been influenced by the Christ. Jesus knows them and they will know him when they die. God is merciful and they will receive mercy. This is the teaching of all the major Christian denominations. This has been described as pious pagans. Jesus knows his own no matter what their culture.

Those who called themselves Christians who did not follow Jesus are hypocrites, and the Gospel shows Jesus having little use for hypocrites. Putting on a display of being religious may deceive everybody, but God is not fooled. Jesus displays little tolerance for hypocrites in the Gospels. Hypocrites do great damage to the image of the church by disillusioning people as to the integrity of the faith. They will also get what they were seeking apart from God. God sees through the mask of self-righteousness they wear.

Punishment means to suffer for some offense committed. God does not inflict this suffering on these lost souls. God allows them to suffer the consequences of their actions. God's justice is perfect. They are reaping what they sowed in life. God desires all people would come to heaven. God desires all people accept salvation, but God allows us the freedom to receive or reject the love of Jesus Christ. This is the judgment. This is what determines our eternal fate. Our heavenly Father, even more than a human parent, grieves every person who rejects God's love. One of the major revelations of God in the Judeo-Christian Bible and in the revelation of Jesus Christ is God's emotions. God is not divine apathy as the Greek stoics imagined. God is an intensely loving parent. God pursues all the children to come home, and too many run from God. They have made their choice. There is great joy in heaven when the sinner returns to the fold.

Conviction of Sin

How we judge ourselves is a critical factor in determining our eternal judgment. Our acceptance of Jesus as our Savior is a problem of good conscience. It is typical of our pridefulness that we try to deceive ourselves that we are good people. Before we even consider the possibility of needing a Savior, we have to acknowledge there is something terribly wrong in our lives. Without an intimate relationship with God in our lives, there is a void in the center of our being which we frantically attempt to fill with transitory things that never succeed in diminishing that hole in our soul. We seek material possession that promises to make us happy. We chase after sexual gratification that promises pleasure and affirmation of our being something. We barricade ourselves from the emptiness within us with greed, narcissism, and lust for power. None of these ever satisfy for long. We use alcohol and drugs to stupefy ourselves into not facing our hollowness. We even go to the extreme of denying God so that we can make ourselves a god. This self-adoration is doomed to fail. Such a little god as our self is pathetic. We have all sinned in some way of intentionally separating ourselves from God. This alienation produces underlying guilt and shame. We begin to believe our own delusions. We become slaves to sin. Our lives can become out of control and headed for destruction.

The judgment we pronounce on ourselves can be devastating, but there is a solution and that is to turn from our wrongs and ask God for forgiveness. We find that forgiveness in Jesus on the cross. If we are sincere, we are forgiven, and that is the end of it. Our honest self-examination leads us to painful self-condemnation, then to redirection of our lives, and culminating in forgiveness, and appreciation of Jesus. We judged ourselves and discover God did not condemn us to hell or oppress his beloved child; rather, God freed us with forgiveness. In a sense, God tells us we have already suffered for our offenses. When you consider God's therapeutic methods, they are so compassionate and wise. To confess and be forgiven produces joy and healing. The process can be painful, but that distress is well worth enduring for the reward of being liberated from the alienation from God. There are times when we cannot do this journey alone and must rely on the support of others. God provides us support for this journey if we seek it. The church is the chosen instrument for the reconciliation of all sinners. It has been said, "The church is not a museum of saints, rather, the church is a hospital for sinners." Our judgment is the path to wholeness and reconciliation with God for us and our brothers and sisters.

How do we Judge

Jesus said in Matthew 7:1-2 (NRSV), "Do not judge, so that you may not be judged. For with the judgment you make you will be judged, and the measure you give will be the measure you get." There is reciprocity in judging others. This warns us to be very cautious about how we judge others. This is more complicated than it appears because we are required to make judgments all the time. Teachers, dog catchers, doctors, cooks, lawyers, farmers, politicians, factory worker, servers, bakers, and florists etc. make judgments as part of their vocations. Of course, that is what they are paid to do. So when is judging appropriate and when is it wrong?

Judging is appropriate when it helps another person become a better person. The caution is that helping is a very delicate business, because it is very easy to do harm to others even when our intentions are to do good. We need to look into ourselves to determine where are our judgments are coming from, and are they valid. There has to be some factor of trust and mutual respect in a relationship before help is offered or received. In extreme situations, help may be incarceration or some form of restraint. This is helping when a person is out of control. This should be obvious to any reasonable person. It is our moral obligation to be aware of and stop destructive behavior. Jesus is not an anarchist. On the contrary, Jesus calls us to the highest standards of morality. The difficult decision is what is our responsibility to inject our sense of morality on others and when do we need to be tolerant of others. We could read hundreds of books on current moral issues and still not cover the topic of moralities. We face issues of large and small of morality daily. There are thousands of moral issues facing us, so where do we find the answers? The reliable sources are the Bible, the church, the law, our Christian mentors, and the Holy Spirit. We must be well informed and compassionately consider different points of view before we rush to judgment. Jesus tells us to be very deliberate on how we judge others. Too often, we are critical of another's failing while ignoring our own glaring faults. In Matthew 7:3 (NRSV), "Why do you see the speck in your neighbor's eye, but do not notice the log in your own eye?" Our ultimate guide is to decide, what is the most loving thing to do? Ignoring a situation is never the loving thing to do. Compassion requires some response. Jesus is our ultimate standard on moral questions.

CHAPTER 16

ETERNAL LIFE

Eternal life is to be in the presence of God, in God's reality, in God's time. This is time without boundaries. In God's time, everything is present, and everything is now. Eternal life is not our concept of time, moments extended into an endless duration. Eternal life is an entirely different concept of time, completely different than time as we think we know it. God's time is the eternal now.

Our experience of time is a succession of moments, like a line that is an endless succession of points streaming to infinity. We experience life from moment to moment, never truly existing in the past or in the future. The past is our memories colored by our emotions immediately receding from our grasp. The future only exists in our imagination, tantalizingly beyond our grasp. The present, the moment that we exist in, moves so rapidly it is almost imperceptible. The present moment is the fleeting now where the eternal is accessible. But in our perception of time, the present flies by us like the view out the window of a speeding vehicle. On rare occasions, we have a sensation of time expanding, such as an extreme crisis when the adrenaline is pumping through our veins. Time seems to almost stop during an accident. In those rare moments when we are connected with the Holy One, we may experience being outside of the normal perception of time. Contemplative prayer helps us dwell for a brief period in the eternal now.

Eternal life is living in the present moment, the eternal now. Past, present, and future are all in the present moment. In the eternal life with God, one can move through time with the ease that one can move through a room. All time co-exists to the individual and is no longer linear; rather, time is multidimensional. If one were to imagine linear time as drops of water lined up, then eternal life with God is like being in the ocean deep. Time and space exist in every direction and we only chose which direction we want to perceive. When we leave this physical universe, we move to a different dimension where all the laws of physics we think we know no longer exist, and we learn to adjust to a whole new understanding of reality. Fortunately, there is ample opportunity and companions to make the adjustment to this higher reality. Our understanding of "reality" is the culmination of what we have experienced. When we move into the eternal, we have to let go of what we have learned in life and graduate to a higher reality. We develop from our limited consciousness toward God consciousness.

In this world, we are prisoners of time. Time is too often our enemy. In eternal life, time is a medium that we move through as easily as we move through air. Time is no longer our enemy; rather, it is simply a medium we move through. To God, everything is present and one. When we are with God, we exist in the presence of everything. There can be no other way, because we are in God's reality. Our physical universe and God's world could not be more different. God created our universe to be relatively simple for God's children. The laws of this physical universe do not exist in God's world. The place where God is has its own spiritual laws. God's world is infinitely complex. As energy, mass, and space govern the physical universe, love, hope, and faith govern heaven. To be in harmony with God in love, hope, and faith is holiness. God is the spiritual law of the heavenly world. Heaven manifests the nature of God where all is beautiful, good, and perfect.

Love is the overriding principle that controls everything in heaven. Time and space do not exist as we know them. What we love is what moves us through heaven. Our ability to love draws us to the infinite possibilities that exist in heaven. Love is relational. Everything that is good, everything that is beautiful, and everything that is godly exists in heaven. The ultimate expression of love is to be in the very presence of God. Anything that we want to know, we can experience, and we will know it. Every good thing that we want to feel, we can feel, and we will know it. Every good thing that we want to be, we can be it. In heaven we are continually growing in perfection. This perfection is to be in perfect relationship with God and to be holy. Holiness means to be in perfect relationship with God. We do not lose our identity in heaven; in fact, it is the unique gift that we have to give to God. To develop in uniqueness and to be in perfect concord with God is why we were created. As we grow in holiness, we grow in our awareness of the glory of God. To be fully present and in the glory of God, the presence of God, is only for those who have become perfectly holy. There cannot be even a speck of a shadow of doubt in the presence of the glory of God. We will only go into the glorious presence of God when we have achieved perfect Holiness, perfect love. That process of sanctification is begun in this world and is completed in heaven. It will happen at the exact rate necessary. There are many levels to heaven, and we move through these levels towards intimacy with God as our progress toward complete holiness dictates. We will succeed eventually because it is the plan of God and the reason why we were created.

Human eye has not seen nor did imagination envision what God has in store for us when we go to heaven. Christians trust the promise that we will be taken to heaven by Jesus Christ. "In my Father's house there are many dwelling places. If it were not so, would I have told you that I go to prepare a place for you? And if I go and prepare a place for you, I will come again and will take you to myself, so that where I am, there you may be also," John 14:2-3 (NRSV). He will bring with him angels to bring us to heaven. Some of these messengers of God may be family members or friends who have gone on before us and are sent to comfort and greet us. They will appear to us in recognizable form, even though they will be young and beautiful. The surroundings that we are brought into will be specifically for us, so that we will be comfortable and at ease. We will be enveloped and overwhelmed with love, knowing that all of our sins have been forgiven. This is our homecoming since heaven is our true home.

We were created in heaven, and with the exception of our brief life in this world, we are eternal residents of heaven. We are created to be children of God, and this life in the physical world is the birthing of our maturing spiritual being. This life is a classroom, and love is the lesson. When we leave this world, we are becoming who we truly are. Our heavenly home is where we are truly known and greatly loved. It is where we belong and where our deepest longings are satisfied. We will meet Jesus Christ, stand before him, and he will look into our eyes. Paul writes, "For now we see in a mirror, dimly, but then we will see face to face. Now I know only in part; then I will know fully, even as I have been fully known," 1 Corinthians 13:12 (NRSV). When we stand before Jesus, we will be before all knowledge, all truth, and all love. We will be aware of the atonement of Christ on the cross and how he has made us acceptable in heaven. What we never understood will be perfectly clear and we will be filled with joy and reverence.

All of our life in this world has been for the moment when we might hear Jesus say, "Well done, good and trustworthy slave," Matthew 25:21 (NRSV). This is the goal of life. It is not a mystery why we are born in this world. Our lives are all preparation for this moment which is the beginning of our life in eternity. What we will feel and know is beyond words.

There are so many new things to adjust to in heaven that we will initially be learning the new realities of our heavenly home. There will be ample opportunity to meet anyone that we would like to meet from the entire history of the world. There is an infinite variety of things to learn and things to do, but the most important work is to continue our transformation into the holy children of God we were created to be. This will be our purification, and because of our intense desire to be with our Creator, we will earnestly strive for holiness. Jesus Christ and all the Saints will guide us and support us until we arrived at the ultimate glory of God.

In eternal life, we will never be bored, we will never be tired, and we will never grieve because "we know that all things work together for good for those who love God, who are called according to his purpose," Romans 8:28 (NRSV). We will understand God's plan for everyone and why it has to be the way it is. There will be no tears, no regrets, and no turning back.

In heaven, our ascent toward the glory of the presence of God will be joyous since we know to whom we belong and where we are going. In this world, our spiritual development has been difficult. All have suffered in this life and felt desolation. This is not the case in heaven. When we understand the reasons for our trials in this world, we find them not just bearable but appreciate them for the outcome of the good that resulted. This is so wonderfully explained in the following scripture: "Blessed be the God and Father of our Lord Jesus Christ! By his great mercy he has given us a new birth into a living hope through the resurrection of Jesus Christ from the dead, and into an inheritance that is imperishable, undefiled, and unfading, kept in heaven for you, who are being protected by the power of God through faith for a salvation ready to be revealed in the last time. In this you rejoice, even if now for a little while you have had to suffer various trials, so that the genuineness of your faith—being more precious than gold that, though perishable, is tested by fire—may be found to result in praise and glory and honor when Jesus Christ is revealed. Although you have not seen him, you love him; and even though you do not see him now, you believe in him and rejoice with an indescribable and glorious joy, for you are receiving the outcome of your faith, the salvation of your souls," 1 Peter 1:3-9 (NRSV). We anticipate our journey towards perfect holiness in this world and into eternal life with joyful expectation of good beyond measure.

The ultimate destiny for humans is to go into the presence of the glory of God. This experience is ineffable. We joined with God to participate in the ongoing act of creation. The heavenly host is like a symphony orchestra that continually praises God and participates with God in the creation. Each person brings their unique individual gifts to the symphony, as each musician has their unique instrument and talents to bring to the orchestra. Our life experience, unique soul, and love of God are the contribution that we make to the symphony. God is the composer and conductor of the orchestra, and we have the privilege of being his instruments, contributing our gift to the glory of the Creator. This is the music of the spheres that makes all time and space possible. Without this music, there would be no time or space, no energy or matter, no universes, nothing at all. All that exists in the physical universe is composed of these vibrations. Our destiny is to become one with the maker of all things.

Heaven rejoices when the lost soul is found. Jesus said, "Just so, I tell you, there will be more joy in heaven over one sinner who repents than over ninety-nine righteous persons who need no repentance," Luke 15:7 (NRSV). God wants all people to come to heaven, but all people do not want to go to heaven. God would never force a person to come to heaven. In fact, a person must desire the love of God more than anything else in order to go to heaven. We cannot buy our way into heaven with our deeds. The only admission into heaven is what Jesus taught from the Torah. "'You shall love the Lord your God with all your heart, and with all your soul, and with all your mind.' This is the greatest and first commandment. And a second is like it: 'You shall love your neighbor as yourself,'" Matthew 22:37-39 (NRSV). This is the way, the truth, and the life of Jesus Christ. This is the only way to heaven. God and Christ are One (John 17:11) and there is no way around the Holy One. Those who do not choose this way are repelled by the love of God, repelled by the love of Jesus Christ, and repelled by the love of heaven. They go away from God and this is how they end up in the outer darkness. May the Lord have mercy on their souls.

CHAPTER 17

SALVATION

When a person genuinely accepts Jesus Christ as their Lord and Savior, they are changed. More precisely, they are beginning a transformation toward holiness. How wonderful it would be if the individual were magically turned into a saint, but that is not how it works. This process of sanctification takes more than our lifetime in this world. We continue our process of sanctification in heaven, and that takes as long as necessary. No one is perfect except Jesus Christ. No one is without sin except Jesus Christ. In fact, as we begin to have an ever-increasing awareness of the holiness of God, we become painfully aware of our own corruption. Thankfully, we are accompanied by the Holy Spirit who also makes known the forgiveness we receive through Jesus Christ. In salvation, we experience a love that is different than the love we knew. There are occasions when we have known God's love prior to salvation, but the intensity and magnitude of God's love is beyond human love. We seek means to share this love with others, because our cup overflows with love. We are eager to express this new experience of love, and often we are rejected because it is misunderstood. Hopefully, we find appropriate ways to express this love in a church community. Salvation is a dramatic journey which has may twists and turns. It is not the smooth sailing we first imagine.

All the defeats and successes are growth opportunities toward holiness. When you closely examine the lives of saintly persons, you find they fought the good fight, and it was never easy. Once on the path of salvation, it would be almost impossible to turn back.

The Gift of Salvation
Salvation is a gift offered to all people through faith in Jesus Christ. People may speculate about who is saved and who is not, but the Bible is explicit about who they are. According to the Gospels, salvation is given to those people who give their lives to Jesus Christ. This is the inspired word of God in the Bible, and anything else is pure speculation. If you want the assurance that you are going to heaven, this is the only way that you can have that total assurance. Jesus came into this world to save you, and he is patiently waiting for your response to his love. In John 3:17-18 (NRSV), we read, "Indeed, God did not send the Son into the world to condemn the world, but in order that the world might be saved through him. Those who believe in him are not condemned; but those who do not believe are condemned already, because they have not believed in the name of the only Son of God." The choice is yours to make and it will have eternal consequences. This is not about religious dogma. It is entirely about your relationship with the chosen one of God, Jesus the Christ.

What must Happen to the Saved?
There have been countless teachers, prophets, gurus, religions, cults, and other philosophies about the path to God. None of these can promise you eternal life except one. Only faith in Jesus can assure you of eternity in heaven. He said, "I am the way, and the truth, and the life. No one comes to the Father except through me," John 14:6 (NRSV). This statement clearly states the unity of God and Jesus. This statement is made in a whole discourse from Jesus about the relationship of God and Jesus. There have been so many paths and there will continue to be many old and new ways,

but there is only one certain way to God. There have been many teachers and prophets, but there has only been the One Son of God. There have been, and continue to be, vast numbers of religions, but there is only one truth that will take you to God. There are infinite numbers of choices in a lifetime, but there is only one choice that will get you to heaven. We find in John 10:7-10 (NRSV), "Jesus said to them, 'Very truly, I tell you, I am the gate for the sheep. All who came before me are thieves and bandits; but the sheep did not listen to them. I am the gate. Whoever enters by me will be saved, and will come in and go out and find pasture. The thief comes only to steal and kill and destroy. I came that they may have life, and have it abundantly.'" The salvation that Jesus offers is abundant life, new life, the fullness of life in this world, and eternal life with God. It is not about pie in the sky in the great by-and-by. The salvation that Jesus gives begins the day you accept him.

Many people have had some acquaintance with Christianity, but they have not given themselves to Jesus. Often times, they have flirted with new and different ways to God. They are promiscuous in their faith. From his love, Jesus warns us about infidelity. In Luke 13:23-24 (NRSV), "Someone asked him, 'Lord, will only a few be saved?' He said to them, 'Strive to enter through the narrow door; for many, I tell you, will try to enter and will not be able.'" With the ever-increasing opportunities for communication in the global community, there is an explosion of new religious opportunities being taught. It is impossible for one person to keep up with the latest fads, revelations, and gurus. Is this possibly a sign of the end of the age? In Matthew 24:4-5 (NRSV), "Jesus answered them, 'Beware that no one leads you astray. For many will come in my name, saying, "I am the Messiah!" and they will lead many astray.'" And in Matthew 24:10-13 (NRSV), "Then many will fall away, and they will betray one another and hate one another. And many false prophets will arise and lead many astray. And because of the increase of lawlessness, the love of many will grow cold. But the one who endures to the end will be saved." Christianity is in alarming decline in Europe and North America. Europe is now referred to as post-Christian and the United States is not far behind. The common belief that the developed nations are predominantly Christian is false. The developed countries' dominant belief is materialism. How many of the faithful will in endure to the end? Former Christian nations are losing their salvation.

<u>The Eyes are Opened</u>
In the hymn "Amazing Grace," it states, "I once was lost, but now am found; was blind, but now I see." The day of salvation is when the spiritually blind see for the first time through the eyes of faith. The following story from the ministry of Jesus was told to illustrate this: Luke 18:35-43 (NRSV), "As he approached Jericho, a blind man was sitting by the roadside begging. When he heard a crowd going by, he asked what was happening. They told him, 'Jesus of Nazareth is passing by.' Then he shouted, 'Jesus, Son of David, have mercy on me!' Those who were in front sternly ordered him to be quiet; but he shouted even more loudly, 'Son of David, have mercy on me!' Jesus stood still and ordered the man to be brought to him; and when he came near, he asked him, 'What do you want me to do for you?' He said, 'Lord, let me see again.' Jesus said to him, 'Receive your sight; your faith has saved you.' Immediately he regained his sight and followed him, glorifying God; and all the people, when they saw it, praised God." For many people who did not know Jesus, meeting him for the first time is like having your eyes open to the world that was never seen before. Without the insight that he gives, we see the world in little episodes that appear to be random and confusing. When the Spirit of Christ lives in us, the pieces of the puzzle come together and we begin to see the whole picture from a new perspective. We begin to see the world through Jesus' eyes and through his understanding. Living without the Spirit of Christ in us is living in isolation without seeing our connection to God and seeing our connection to our brothers and sisters. With the Spirit of Christ, we begin to know how important

we are to God and how important our relationships are to one another. Our lives are no longer a series of random accidents. We see for the first time that every moment is significant and part of a divine plan. The blind man immediately began to worship God for two reasons: He gave God the glory because he was given the gift of sight, and he knew for the first time how much God loved him. This is the model for how we respond to our salvation, by first worshiping God and giving God the glory.

Our second response to receiving salvation is to change the course of our lives in meaningful ways. We are no longer content to live as we have lived, so we critically examine our past and seek to make amends. In Luke 19:1-10 (NRSV), "He entered Jericho and was passing through it. A man was there named Zacchaeus; he was a chief tax collector and was rich. He was trying to see who Jesus was, but on account of the crowd he could not, because he was short in stature. So he ran ahead and climbed a sycamore tree to see him, because he was going to pass that way. When Jesus came to the place, he looked up and said to him, 'Zacchaeus, hurry and come down; for I must stay at your house today.' So he hurried down and was happy to welcome him. All who saw it began to grumble and said, 'He has gone to be the guest of one who is a sinner.' Zacchaeus stood there and said to the Lord, 'Look, half of my possessions, Lord, I will give to the poor; and if I have defrauded anyone of anything, I will pay back four times as much.' Then Jesus said to him, 'Today salvation has come to this house, because he too is a son of Abraham. For the Son of Man came to seek out and to save the lost.'" Zacchaeus not only received Jesus as his Savior but immediately responded to his salvation by using half of his money to help the poor, repay his debts extravagantly, and rebuild relationships with his neighbors. Zacchaeus was part of a corrupt government that exploited the conquered people of Israel for the avarice of Rome. He acquired wealth by extorting money from the exploited. His announcement that he would pay back fourfold those he defrauded is his awareness of the corrupt system he had been a part of. Salvation gives us new insight into the corruption of the world around us. It is a shock to see what we have participated in prior to our salvation. Salvation has real consequences in our lives. When we have truly received the gift of salvation that Jesus offers us, we want to follow him forever. Being his disciple is not easy and it is not cheap. Reconciliation with God is not cheap grace.

The Cross in Salvation

The way, the truth, and the life of Christ is the most rewarding and the most difficult path that one can take. In Matthew 16:24-26 (NRSV), we read, "Then Jesus told his disciples, 'If any want to become my followers, let them deny themselves and take up their cross and follow me. For those who want to save their life will lose it, and those who lose their life for my sake will find it. For what will it profit them if they gain the whole world but forfeit their life? Or what will they give in return for their life?'" The reward is immediate because we know that everything works together for God's good purpose for those who love God. The value of the transitory things of this world cannot compare to the value of the eternal things that we strive for in following Jesus. What motivated us before we knew Jesus are mere temptations. What motivates a follower of Christ is to serve him and to please him in thought, word, and deed. Taking up the cross of Christ, although difficult, is a joy that exceeds any rational understanding, because love of Jesus is beyond words. What one is willing to do for love cannot be explained in words. The cross is the symbol of salvation. To the Christian, the cross is the glory of God.

Obstacles to Grace

The obstacles we erect to the gift of salvation that Jesus offers are many. We refuse salvation because of pride in our independence. We refuse salvation because of our low self-esteem because we think we are not worthy. We refuse salvation because we're distracted by the enticements of this world. The love of money is a great distraction.

Read in Matthew 19:23-26 (NRSV), "Then Jesus said to his disciples, 'Truly I tell you, it will be hard for a rich person to enter the kingdom of heaven. Again I tell you, it is easier for a camel to go through the eye of a needle than for someone who is rich to enter the kingdom of God.' When the disciples heard this, they were greatly astounded and said, 'Then who can be saved?' But Jesus looked at them and said, 'For mortals it is impossible, but for God all things are possible.'" There is a strange phenomenon in human nature called greed: the more we have, the more we want. Those of us who have been blessed with wealth seem to lose all appreciation for the wealth that we have, and instead we become obsessed with acquiring more wealth. The lust for money drives so many away from the love of God. How many people have lost their souls because of their craving for the temporal things of this world? Alcoholism, drug addiction, greed, sex addiction, and the love of money are a few of the barriers that we create which become insurmountable obstacles to salvation.

Jesus warns us about the barriers to salvation because it is his desire that all people would be saved, but he also knows that many people will refuse the gift of forgiveness and salvation. The parable of the seed is explained by Jesus to his disciples because it is imperative that we understand it. In Luke 8:11-15 (NRSV), we read, "Now the parable is this: The seed is the word of God. The ones on the path are those who have heard; then the devil comes and takes away the word from their hearts, so that they may not believe and be saved. The ones on the rock are those who, when they hear the word, receive it with joy. But these have no root; they believe only for a while and in a time of testing fall away. As for what fell among the thorns, these are the ones who hear; but as they go on their way, they are choked by the cares and riches and pleasures of life, and their fruit does not mature. But as for that in the good soil, these are the ones who, when they hear the word, hold it fast in an honest and good heart, and bear fruit with patient endurance." If we're faithful followers of Jesus Christ and have received him, we will be living fruitful lives. There is evidence of our faith by what God has accomplished through us. We glorify God in being willing instruments of his work of love and reconciliation to all people. We will be known by our fruits. How has God been glorified in our lives?

The Plan of Salvation

God has never abandon humankind. In God's plan of salvation, we are at the threshold of the decision, for today is the day of salvation. In Jesus, God's plan has been perfectly revealed. There is no longer any mystery or confusion if you are willing to accept what God wants to give you. Jesus is the Chosen One to lead us to salvation.

We find Jesus saying in John 4:22-26 (NRSV), "'You worship what you do not know; we worship what we know, for salvation is from the Jews. But the hour is coming, and is now here, when the true worshipers will worship the Father in spirit and truth, for the Father seeks such as these to worship him. God is spirit, and those who worship him must worship in spirit and truth.' The woman said to him, 'I know that Messiah is coming' (who is called Christ). 'When he comes, he will proclaim all things to us.' Jesus said to her, 'I am he, the one who is speaking to you.'" Jesus speaks to us through the entire Bible, through the Holy Spirit in our prayers, and through the proclamation of the church. You can ignore him if you choose. But if you have ears to listen and eyes to see, you will know that he is speaking to you. He speaks to us softly and tenderly, calling sinners to come home.

Once Jesus was in the home of a righteous man, a woman came and adored him. Some of the guests were horrified that he would allow a despised sinner to touch him and be welcomed in his presence. They complained about her being in their presence. Jesus spoke to them saying, "'Therefore, I tell you, her sins, which were many, have been forgiven; hence she has shown great love. But the one to whom little is forgiven, loves little.' Then he said to her, 'Your sins are forgiven.' But those who were at the table with him began to say among themselves, 'Who is this who even forgives sins?' And he said to the woman, 'Your faith has saved you; go in peace,'" Luke 7:47-50 (NRSV). No matter how terrible you may think your sins are, Jesus is ready to forgive you and welcome you into the kingdom of God. As he forgave this fallen woman, he is eager to forgive you. When you ask him to forgive your sins and to dwell in your heart, you will know how real he is.

Jesus Christ is the Word of God, which is the truth, and the way of eternal life. Our salvation depends on whether we have accepted and lived according to the Word of God. The judgment is not a debate or trial, because in the light of God, there is only the truth and there is not even a hint of the shadow of deception. How do our lives compare to or contradict the Word of God? That is the judgment. Have we received forgiveness for our sins, have we received the word of God in Jesus Christ, and have we been obedient to his commandments? Everyone knows in their heart the answers to these questions. Jesus said we are responsible for our lives and our salvation. In John 12:47-48 (NRSV), "I do not judge anyone who hears my words and does not keep them, for I came not to judge the world, but to save the world. The one who rejects me and does not receive my word has a judge; on the last day the word that I have spoken will serve as judge." May you know his great love and hope for you today.

CHAPTER 18

THE KINGDOM OF GOD

The "Kingdom of God" is where God reigns in heaven and on earth. Jesus came to bring the kingdom of God into this world through the hearts and minds of those who would love him and followed his commandments. The kingdom of heaven and the kingdom of God are the same thing. Only those people who love God with all their hearts, all their minds, all their strength, and love their neighbors as themselves will go to heaven. Only those people who have God reigning in their hearts are known to belong in the kingdom of God, and are candidates for the kingdom of heaven. God knows who has the Spirit of God, and God knows this absolutely. Our fate will be decided by this criterion alone. Jesus is the chosen instrument of God to bring the kingdom into this world so that God reigns in every person's heart, mind, and soul.

The Kingdom Comes
In the Kingdom of God, we will be overwhelmed by the love of God as shown to us by the love of Christ. This is the work of Jesus, which is to show us completely the love of God. In the Holiness of Christ's love, we will be profoundly aware of all that we have been forgiven and how terribly we have been flawed as human

beings. Yet we will be completely reassured by the love and acceptance that we receive from Jesus and the Saints that we belong in heaven, and all of our apprehension will vanish in the bliss of being in Christ's presence. We will know that our insufficiency is completely insignificant in the fullness of Jesus. In Luke 12:32 (NRSV), "Do not be afraid, little flock, for it is your Father's good pleasure to give you the kingdom." The day that we are taken to heaven will be the most wondrous and joyful day of our entire existence, and heaven will rejoice at our arrival. Everything we suffered in the world will be inconsequential at that moment. Meeting Jesus, face-to-face, and having him embrace us, will fill us with the love and acceptance that we have never known in this world. And through Jesus, we will be fully known, and we will know everything we have ever wanted to know. For the first time in our experience, everything will be clear and right, and will understand that we have always been a part of God's plan. In Matthew 25:34 (NRSV), "Then the king will say to those at his right hand, 'Come, you that are blessed by my Father, inherit the kingdom prepared for you from the foundation of the world.'" When we leave this world, our conscious understanding of who we are is the same as what we were in this world, but as we begin to accept and appreciate who we really are, the perishable will put on the imperishable. We will become transformed into our eternal bodies as radiant beings of light. We will have new bodies that are not made of matter as we know it; instead, we will have spiritual bodies that shine like the sun. In Matthew 13:43 (NRSV), "Then the righteous will shine like the sun in the kingdom of their Father." As we become perfected in heaven, we will come to know that we were created for a purpose, which is to serve God in heaven. He created us to participate in the creative and loving process of being in God's eternity. In Luke 22:29 (NRSV), Jesus says to his disciples, "And I confer on you, just as my Father has conferred on me, a kingdom." We will join with the angels, all the saints, Jesus Christ, and God in the ongoing creation of world.

We will share in the spiritual intimacy of God's great love and live as one in ultimate bliss of God's kingdom. Jesus says in Luke 22:30 (NRSV), "So that you may eat and drink at my table in my kingdom, and you will sit on thrones judging the twelve tribes of Israel." In compassion for this world that we have left behind, we will pray for our brothers and sisters to accept the grace of God so that they might also come to heaven.

Entry into the Kingdom
The Kingdom of God is for those people who have put their trust in God and Jesus who is the one that God sent to bring all people to heaven. When a person puts their faith in Jesus, they become like a little child who has complete faith and trust in their parents. The little children were rushing toward Jesus to be with him, and his disciples tried to stop them. Matthew 19:14 reads, "Jesus said, 'Let the little children come to me, and do not stop them; for it is to such as these the kingdom of heaven belongs.'" We must have the complete love and faith of a child so that we accept him completely. The trust and faith of a child is where we may have started in life and possibly lost that faith as we grew. Who was responsible for our loss of faith? Our faith may have been ruined by someone we trusted. In Mark 10:15 (NRSV), Jesus said, "Truly I tell you, whoever does not receive the kingdom of God as a little child will never enter it." In our lives, we often become overwhelmed with the cares and worries of this world. These worldly concerns can be the impediment to following the commandments of Jesus. Jesus was very aware of this problem and told us we cannot be obsessed with our material needs, but we must stay focused on what is really important in this life. In our materialistic culture, this spiritual perspective is difficult to attain. In Matthew 6:33 (NRSV), Jesus says, "But strive first for the kingdom of God and his righteousness, and all these things will be given to you as well." All things of this world are transitory, and we should not lose our eternal soul by worrying about worldly needs to the neglect of God's will.

Status in the Kingdom

Who is the greatest in the Kingdom of Heaven? Jesus has some big surprises for us, some concerning status in the kingdom of heaven. The way that we think of the world is not the way that God thinks of the world, and we are all in for some big surprises when we go to heaven. Some of the most exalted people in this world will be lowly in heaven, and the humble people that were probably invisible to us will be the most exalted in heaven. In Matthew 18:4 (NRSV), "Whoever becomes humbles like this child is the greatest in the kingdom of heaven." Jesus, over and over again, teaches us that it is in the doing of his commandments that we please and glorify God. It is also in the teaching of these commandments that God is glorified. Perverting the commandments of Christ displeases God. In Matthew 5:19 (NRSV), "Therefore, whoever breaks one of the least of these commandments, and teaches others to do the same, will be called least in the kingdom of heaven; but whoever does them and teaches them will be called great in the kingdom of heaven." The very least one in the kingdom of God is greater than any human on this earth. Jesus states many times in the Gospels, "The first shall be last and the last shall be first." We better not think too highly of ourselves. It would be better to be the lowliest being in heaven than to be the greatest human on this planet. In Luke 7:28 (NRSV), "I tell you, among those born of women no one is greater than John; yet the least in the kingdom of God is greater than he." We will be amazed in heaven at the diversity of people who are there, who have loved Jesus, and who have followed his commandments. We have such a narrow-minded understanding of the global scope of the faith of Jesus Christ that we will be surprised by our brothers and sisters and Christ of whom we were completely unaware. There are people who have known the Spirit of Christ who we have not recognized as our brothers and sisters and Christ. The Spirit of Christ has been working in the world since the beginning of time, often in ways that we do not understand. In Luke 13:29 (NRSV), "Then people will come from east and west, from north and south, and will eat in the kingdom of God." The kingdom of heaven will be the most interesting, diverse group, and stimulating experience beyond anything we have ever known in this world. Heaven is the centerpiece of all creation and everything that is good, beautiful, and holy is in heaven. It is the supreme goal of every rational being to go to heaven.

There are three births in our life's journey towards the kingdom of heaven. The first is when we are born into this world, the second is when we are born from above into the Spirit of God, and the third is when we are born into heaven. When we invite Jesus Christ to be our Savior and we put our faith and trust in him, we are becoming a new person. This does not happen instantly but we begin a process of sanctification that will radically change the course of our life. In John 3:3 (NRSV), "Jesus answered him, 'Very truly I tell you, no one can see the kingdom of God without being born from above.'" To be born from above is to begin to die to the old way of life and to be reborn into a new way of life. This is symbolically reenacted in the Sacrament of Baptism where a person goes into the water of death and is reborn into the life of the Spirit. Jesus gave us this Sacrament of Baptism for the individual to join into the community of believers by showing their symbolic death and a rebirth. In John 3:5 (NRSV), "Jesus answered, 'Very truly I tell you, no one can enter the kingdom of God without being born of water and the Spirit.'" If a person is sincere in their desire to renounce their old way of life and receive Jesus Christ as their new way of life, the Sacrament of Baptism within the community of the church establishes them as a new member of the Body of Christ.

According to the teachings of Jesus, there are a number of signs you are near the Kingdom of God. A follower of Jesus would like to know whether they are on the right course or are they deceiving themselves. Jesus has given us some clear statements about who belongs in the kingdom of God. In Matthew 5:3 (NRSV), "Blessed are the poor in spirit, for theirs is the kingdom of heaven." Those who yearn for and are hungry for the Spirit of God are those who will receive the kingdom of God. In Matthew 5:10 (NRSV), "Blessed are those who are persecuted for righteousness' sake, for theirs is the kingdom of heaven." As Jesus was persecuted for his righteousness, so will those who follow his commandments be persecuted for their righteousness. In Mark 12:34 (NRSV), "When Jesus saw that he had answered wisely, he said to him, 'You are not far from the kingdom of God.'" A person who has wisdom from the scriptures is not far from the kingdom of God. Jesus said in Luke 8:10 (NRSV), "To you have been given the knowledge of the secrets of the kingdom of God, but to others I speak in parables, so that, 'looking they may not perceive, and listening they may not understand.'" The word of God can only be understood through the inspiration of the Spirit of God, and a person inspired by the Holy Spirit learns the secrets of the kingdom. In Luke 12:31 (NRSV), "Instead strive for his kingdom, and these things will be given to you as well." If one lives by the Spirit and seeks the kingdom of God, our material and worldly needs will not be of primary importance to us.

Jesus gave us warning signs that we may be far from the Kingdom of God. There are many people in this world who claim they are Christians, but there is very little evidence in their lives that they obey the commandments of Jesus. If they were on trial for being a Christian, would there be enough evidence to convict them? The demons knew Jesus was the Son of God, and their belief in him did not qualify them for the kingdom of heaven. Just because a person says they believe in Jesus does not make them a follower of Jesus.

The demons believe. The world is full of people who call themselves Christians but there is little proof that they are sincere in the faith. Jesus says in Matthew 7:21 (NRSV), "Not everyone who says to me, 'Lord, Lord,' will enter the kingdom of heaven, but only the one who does the will of my Father in heaven." A very good indication that a person is a genuine follower of Jesus is that their life produces results in the building up of the church, spreading the Gospel, and ministering in the name of Christ. In Matthew 21:43 (NRSV), Jesus says, "Therefore I tell you, the kingdom of God will be taken away from you and given to a people that produces the fruits of the kingdom."

Humans judge by the appearances they see, but God judges by what is in a person's heart. We judge superficially and our judgment is not God's judgment. In Matthew 21:31 (NRSV), "Jesus said to them, 'Truly I tell you, the tax collectors and the prostitutes are going into the kingdom of God ahead of you.'" Our righteousness is but filthy rags compared to the righteousness of God. Many sinners who have repented of their sin will go to heaven before the people that they think are so righteous. Jesus uses hyperbole to emphasize the necessity for scrupulously examining our own sin, and casting and it out of our lives. For example, Mark 9:47 (NRSV), "And if your eye causes you to stumble, tear it out; it is better for you to enter the kingdom of God with one eye than to have two eyes and be thrown into hell." Jesus takes the problem of sin seriously because it is alienation from God and that is our damnation.

The love of money is one of the causes of sin in our materialistic society. People's lust for money keeps them from being charitable, supporting the work of the Body of Christ, and obeying the commandments of Christ. In Mark 10:23-25 (NRSV), "Then Jesus looked around and said to his disciples, 'How hard it will be for those who have wealth to enter the kingdom of God!' And the disciples were perplexed at these words. But Jesus said to them again, 'Children, how hard it is to enter the kingdom of God! It is easier for a camel to go through the eye of a needle than for someone who is rich to enter the kingdom of God.'" Fortunately for us, Jesus tells us that it is possible for a rich man to enter the kingdom of God, because for God all things are possible. This is a serious warning to those who are rich about the lust for money to be their downfall.

Anyone who teaches, preaches, or expresses their opinion about Christianity had better be very cautious about what they say and who they said it to, because what Jesus said to the Pharisees is equally applicable to every Christian. Jesus said in Matthew 23:13 (NRSV), "Woe to you, scribes and Pharisees, hypocrites! For you lock people out of the kingdom of heaven. For you do not go in yourselves, and when others are going in, you stop them." People who are Christians have a responsibility to understand Christianity and not misuse it or misdirect it in any way, because they will be judged for what they have done, and they will not like the consequences of the evil that they have done in the name of Christianity. In Luke 13:28 (NRSV), "There will be weeping and gnashing of teeth when you see Abraham and Isaac and Jacob and all the prophets in the kingdom of God, and you yourselves thrown out."

The coming of the kingdom of God is the Good News of Jesus Christ. From the beginning of his ministry, he preached the arrival of the kingdom of God. In Mark 1:15 (NRSV), "The time is fulfilled, and the kingdom of God has come near; repent, and believe in the good news!" The kingdom of God was truly present in Jesus Christ, and he invited people to accept the Spirit of God in their selves so that the kingdom would be in them. Jesus stated the good news of the kingdom as his primary preaching task and he went about it passionately throughout Israel. In Luke 4:43 (NRSV), "But he said to them, 'I must proclaim the good news of the kingdom of God to the other cities also; for I was sent for this purpose.'" The earthly ministry of Jesus consisted of teaching, preaching the good news of the kingdom, and healing. This is the model for his followers today, to do as Jesus did. We learn in Matthew 9:35 (NRSV), "Then Jesus went about all the cities and villages, teaching in their synagogues, and proclaiming the good news of the kingdom, and curing every disease and every sickness." We are to proclaim the immediacy of God's reign to every person so that the kingdom will become a reality in this world as it is in heaven, and also that each person may have eternal life in the kingdom of heaven. In Matthew 10:7 (NRSV), "As you go, proclaim the good news, 'The kingdom of heaven has come near.'" Jesus tells us that there is urgency in proclaiming the good news, and we are to disregard everything that holds us back from the task at hand. In Luke 9:60 (NRSV), Jesus said, "Let the dead bury their own dead; but as for you, go and proclaim the kingdom of God." Every Christian has a responsibility to proclaim the good news of Jesus Christ. When we follow Jesus, we put our trust in him and he becomes our strength, and the Holy Spirit becomes our thought, word, and deed. We don't dwell in the past of what could've, should've, and would've been. In Luke 9:62 (NRSV), Jesus replied, "No one who puts a hand to the plow and looks back is fit for the kingdom of God." When the message is not received, the Christian moves on to find a receptive audience for the good news of Jesus Christ. We do not waste our time with people who have no interest in Jesus or his salvation. In Luke 10:11 (NRSV), "Even the dust of your town that clings to our feet, we wipe off in protest against you. Yet know this: The kingdom of God has come near." May the Spirit of Christ be in us and may the kingdom of God be proclaimed in all we do.

The kingdom comes to earth through the power of the Holy Spirit working within people who invite the reign of God in their lives. This is an essential part of the prayer that Jesus taught us. We're praying for the kingdom to come and us and into the world. Jesus teaches us to pray in Matthew 6:10 (NRSV), "Your kingdom come. Your will be done, on earth as it is in heaven." Jesus commands that the good news of the kingdom of God be preached throughout the whole world so every person has the chance to accept or deny him. In the past two thousand years, this has not been accomplished, but the time is not far away when the Gospel will have been preached throughout the whole world. When that happens, that may be the end of time as we know it. In Matthew

24:14 (NRSV), "And this good news of the kingdom will be proclaimed throughout the world, as a testimony to all the nations; and then the end will come."

Jesus is the kingdom of heaven and he is king of his kingdom. This world is not his kingdom yet, but will be someday. When that day comes, evil and strife will end in this world. The Christian Church is not the kingdom of God, but it contains people who have the kingdom of God in them, and they are to be a sign to the rest of the world of the kingdom of God. We point to Jesus, we point to God, and we point to heaven. In John 18:36 (NRSV), Jesus said, "My kingdom is not from this world. If my kingdom were from this world, my followers would be fighting to keep me from being handed over to the Jews. But as it is, my kingdom is not from here." The world is full of endless speculation about the end of the world. There is an industry making people rich, predicting the end of the world. It is strange that this has such a following in the Christian Church because the Bible specifically tells us that we will not know when the end will come until it does come. Jesus said in Luke 17:20 (NRSV), "Once Jesus was asked by the Pharisees when the kingdom of God was coming, and he answered, 'The kingdom of God is not coming with things that can be observed.'" The warning signs of the end of the world have been going on for several thousand years and will continue to go on for a little while longer. Jesus tells us that these are birth pangs of the coming of a better world where God will reign in every heart and mind. Mark 13:8 (NRSV) reads, "For nation will rise against nation, and kingdom against kingdom; there will be earthquakes in various places; there will be famines. This is but the beginning of the birth pangs." The second coming of Jesus Christ will happen, and in God's time, and it is our responsibility to be his followers in the here and now without ridiculous speculation about whether the world is going to end today or tomorrow. In Luke 21:31 (NRSV), "So also, when you see these things taking place, you know that the kingdom of God is near." The important question in our lives is not whether we have prophetic visions about the future, but whether we are following Christ to the best of our ability and spreading the good news of Jesus Christ, because the kingdom of God begins with us. In Luke 17:21 (NRSV), "Nor will they say, 'Look, here it is!' or 'There it is!' For, in fact, the kingdom of God is among you."

Jesus taught many parables about the kingdom of heaven. He taught more about this topic than any other, so it must have been of supreme importance to him. The following are a small sample of parables about the kingdom of heaven from the Gospel of Matthew: the parable of the weeds, Matthew 13:24-30; the parable of the mustard seed, Matthew 13:31-32; the parable of the yeast, Matthew 13:33; the parable of the hidden treasure, Matthew 13:44; the parable of the pearl merchant, Matthew 13:45; the parable of the fishing net, Matthew 13:47-50; the parable of the unforgiving debtor, Matthew 18:23-35; the parable of the wedding feast, Matthew 22:2-14; the parable of the ten bridesmaids, Matthew 25:1-13; the parable of the talents, Matthew 25:14-30; and the parable of the workers paid equally, Matthew 20:1-16.

A comprehensive study of the teachings on the kingdom of God would be beyond the scope of this book. To understand Jesus, these teachings need to be studied and understood. Jesus taught the kingdom so that we may be a part of it in this world and in the life after. The kingdom is God's will for us as individuals and collectively for this world if we decide to be part of the kingdom of God. Edward Hicks was an early American preacher and artist. He painted many versions of the "Peaceable Kingdom" during his lifetime. He painted his vision based on Scripture in a simple style of the future of our world. We can only do our best to bring this about and pray the coming of Christ.

CHAPTER 19

THE ENEMY

There is serious opposition to God. The enemies of God take many forms from the blatantly obvious to the seductively subtle. They may be people we know and love. They may be voices in our subconscious from the past and present. They may be demonic spirits. They may be scholars with academic credentials. The adversary comes in all shapes and sizes. They may be in the church and held in high regard. The adversary of God is called "satanas" in Greek. The work of the tempter is always deception. "He is a liar and the father of lies," John 8:44 (NRSV). His purpose is chaos, which is opposition to the plan of God. Jesus and the devil had a constant engagement during Jesus' life in this world and throughout time. The adversary is clever and tireless in his efforts. The power he has in this world is the power we give him. Evil is no match for God, and it is a mistake to equate the devil with God. Evil exists to contrast with good. We are born to distinguish between good and evil. How else would we know good from evil if there were no contrast? The polarity of good and evil is an essential dynamic in spiritual development that makes the world progress. Never become fascinated by evil, but it is critically important that we identify it and stand against it. Evil is worthy of our consideration. Jesus frequently met his opponent directly and defeated him.

Let us examine some of the accusations made against Jesus to see if they are legitimate.

Jesus' Divinity

In any contemporary discussion of Jesus, the denial of Jesus' divinity is going to make an appearance in the conversation because it is so pervasive in our world. The materialistic world view cannot tolerate the concept of the Divine, so it is logical there is no consideration for belief in the divinity of Jesus. The Christian understanding of Jesus as fully human and fully divine is nonsensical to the materialist. There is no room for discussion, which makes Christians delusional from the materialist perspective. Christians are met with scorn and derision by the materialist.

One of the earliest charges against Christians was that Jesus was the bastard son of a Roman soldier. This rumor sought to destroy both Jesus' claim to divinity and legitimacy as a Jew. This rumor based on no evidence was perpetuated for decades amongst his detractors.

The charge brought against Jesus by the Sanhedrin that led to his execution by the Romans was blasphemy. Jesus openly proclaimed he was the Son of God, which was an assertion of his divinity. This was sufficient to warrant the death penalty. There were other motives for the hatred against Jesus, such as Jesus' attack on the corruption of the Temple tax system. Jesus was a serious threat to the established power of the men who cooperated with the Romans in the oppression of the Jews. The reforms of Judaism sought by Jesus were not welcomed by the some of the conservative elements of the religious establishment such as the Pharisees, Sadducees, and scribes.

The concept of Jesus being fully human and fully divine was debated within the early Christian communities and led to several schisms. The prevailing doctrine was ultimately decided at the Council of Nicea in the fourth century. Contrary doctrines were pronounced by the majority of Bishops as anathema.

Jesus was the devil
In the Gospels, there are incidents where the opponents of Jesus accused him of receiving his miraculous powers from a demonic spirit. According to Luke 11:15 (NRSV), "But some of them said, 'He casts out demons by Beelzebul, the ruler of the demons.'" Jesus logically explained to them that this was absurd because why would the ruler of demons destroy demons. This seemed to silence his critics for a time. The demonization of radical Christians has been used to persecute and destroy their movements for the past two thousand years.

Jesus was a false messiah
The time of Jesus was a period of terrible oppression for the people of Israel. There were a number of false messiahs that attempted uprisings against the Roman occupation of Israel. There were false messiahs after Jesus that contributed to the destruction of Israel. In the Hebrew Scriptures, there are several prophetic descriptions of the coming messiah. Jesus met some of these descriptions and was not consistent with other prophecies. For example, Jesus was not a warrior King who would defeat the Romans in warfare. Jesus had no intention of establishing an empire with all the peoples of the world serving the Jewish nation. There is much variation in interpretation of these messianic expectations. No matter how well Jesus coincided with some prophetic Scriptures, there were other Scriptures that contradicted Jesus' ministry. In Israel, there was no consensus about what the Messiah would do.

Jesus was not raised from the dead
The resurrection of Jesus has been debated from the first century to today. It is interesting that one can find in writing unequivocal praise for Jesus, but denial that he was raised from the dead. Some even describe elaborate schemes to substitute another at the crucifixion so that Jesus would survive and appear to his disciples as resurrected. These fictions cunningly make Jesus a charlatan

and a fraud. There is more evidence from multiple sources for Jesus' death and resurrection than almost all other historical reports. The most incontrovertible report of the resurrection comes from Paul, writing two decades after the death and resurrection of Jesus. After the resurrected Christ appeared to the Apostles, Paul writes in 1 Corinthians 15:6 (NRSV), "Then he appeared to more than five hundred brothers and sisters at one time, most of whom are still alive, though some have died." Since this was written while so many of these witnesses were alive and able to support or deny Paul's testimony, it most certainly was reliable. Paul would not rely upon a vast body of witnesses to support the resurrection if there were any doubt about the truth of his claim. Paul received the truth of the resurrection directly from witnesses such as Peter and James within a couple of years after the event. This is as strong historical evidence for the validity of the resurrection as one can get.

Josephus was a Jewish historian who became an apologist for the Roman Empire and acknowledges the miracles and crucifixion of Jesus. The most compelling argument for the truth about Jesus Christ as authentic is the inexplicable devotion of his followers who evangelized throughout the Roman Empire and beyond with extraordinary success. Their faith was based on intimate experiences of the Risen Christ. The Christians conquered the Roman Empire within a few centuries without wealth, political power, an army, and in spite of fierce opposition. There is no rational explanation for this victory over the greatest empire in the history of the world, except that something supernatural happened. That power was the divinity of Jesus alive in his followers. How else can it be explained?

Christians are atheists
The Romans charged Christians with being atheists. This may be curious, but it makes sense from the Roman point of view. The Romans were pantheists and eagerly adopted many gods from

other regions. They even began declaring emperors as gods. So a Roman had to worship the Emperor as well as being obedient. Christians would not worship the Emperor because they considered this a betrayal of Jesus as the Son of God. The result of this refusal to worship the Emperor and declare him lord was that Christians were executed in mass persecutions. This continued periodically for three hundred years. The martyrdom of Christians had the effect of drawing more people to the faith. Christians have also been accused of being pantheists because they hold to the doctrine of the Triune revelation of God. Christians are strictly monotheists but add the Trinitarian understanding to the monotheistic theology.

Christians practice occult rituals
The Romans accused the Christians of human sacrifice, infanticide, and cannibalism. These rumors were based on misunderstanding and distortion of the Lord's Supper. Christians were forced to practice their faith in secret because of the persecutions, so it is understandable that fabrications about their practices would be accepted. How are the mysteries of the Christian faith distorted today in order to discredit Jesus and his followers? It is not uncommon today for critics to describe Christians as cult followers who seek domination of the government. There may be a few fringe Christians who would fit this description, but the overwhelming majority of Christians are not seeking to dominate the government nor are they in cults.

Jesus is one of many masters
The belief that Jesus is just one of many enlightened masters is becoming ever more popular in our society. They are numerous wise teachers and some of them are truly inspired by God, but they are not God. They are men and women who are all flawed humans. One benefits from their wisdom and they may be studied. To accept everything they say without thorough critical examination is

dangerous. We have been given the ability to reason so that we may look critically at everything and logically determine its validity or weaknesses. Study everything that may build us up and take what is of value from it. Dismiss all that is of no value and beware of deception. Jesus is unique and there is none other like him. All religions are not the same, even though one can find similarities. There are vast differences between world religions. Self-proclaimed saviors are never to be trusted except the One.

<ins>Jesus never did miracles and healings</ins>
In our "enlightened" era, anything not based on a materialistic understanding is dismissed as superstition or fantasy. The miracles and healings of Jesus are held in contempt as fraudulent. There are miracles and healings happening all over the world every day, and these are either ignored or called delusions by our cynical world. To the people involved in these miracles and healings, they are well aware that they are not delusional. Lives are miraculously changed by God, and there is no scientific base for explaining these radical transformations. Jesus did many more miracles and healings than are recorded in the Bible and he is doing miracles all around us today. The more we explore the reality of miracles in the world, the more we find. This is the cutting edge of human progress. We deny the power of God at our own peril.

<ins>Jesus enslaves people</ins>
There is a frequent accusation made against Christianity that its followers become caught in a prison of ignorance and superstition. The Christian faith is depicted as "dumbing down." The truly intelligent individual would never indulge in religious thinking. As a superior intellect, religion is beneath any serious consideration, except for anthropological interest. In common language, "you must turn your brain off to have faith in God." Some of the greatest minds in science have believed in God, such as Isaac Newton and Albert Einstein. Intellectual closed mindedness is not a

characteristic of true intelligence. Intellectual curiosity is a critical part of being an intelligent being. Closed mindedness is indicative of fear, insecurity, and pridefulness. Christian faith frees a person from the slavery to sin and death, and they commit themselves to the love of God and to the love of all people. How is this ignorant or closed minded? The real issue is, what are we slavishly following? Is the choice between the path of love or material cynicism?

Jesus damns people to hell
Christianity seeks to save all people from hell. The Bible warns us there are consequences to our actions and we will reap what we sow. Jesus does not condemn people to hell, but he warns us our actions are destructive to the world and to our souls. It is nether loving nor responsible to pretend that everything is good and right. It is not okay to neglect appropriate warnings. In fact, we have warning labels on most things that we purchase. We warn children of danger as responsible adults. We warn drivers of road hazards. Jesus gives us fair warnings about destructive behavior and we need to heed him. He cautions us because he loves us and hopes we will turn our lives around to love. The best teachers are not the most permissive. The best teachers teach the truth. Jesus teaches us to choose the way to heaven or the way to hell.

Jesus never appears to people today
There are thousands of testimonials on the internet by people who have had personal experiences of Jesus, and there are hundreds of books on this subject. One example is the number of near death experiences, which have been coming out in the past few decades. Not all of these are specifically about Jesus, but many are. For all the reported stories about encounters with Jesus, there are many more that go unreported. Many people in the helping professions have been fortunate to receive powerful testimonials from the people they serve about encounters with Jesus. These reports are

extremely emotional, private, and sacred, and often not shared publically. They are very under reported. To those who have seriously investigated these reports of the living Christ, their faith is greatly enhanced.

The testimonies in the Bible about Jesus are false

The Bible is a collection of testimonials. The purpose of these narratives was to propagate the faith. The writers were drawing from personal experience and first person witness. The Gospels were written a few decades after the events occurred because it was necessary to transmit the information in writing because of the limitations of time and travel of the early disciples of Jesus. These testimonials shared the oral traditions of the first disciples and added or excluded material from their body of knowledge about Jesus. The four Gospels each have their own perspective and specific audience which the authors were addressing. They were sincerely attempting to describe the single most world-changing event in human history. Imagine if we had four narratives about the explosion of Mount Vesuvius written by four different individuals. How many differences and similarities would we find? The writers of the Gospels did not benefit from their efforts with money or power; rather, they were risking their lives for their faith. They genuinely transmitted the truth about Jesus to the best of their ability. They intended to propagate the faith with truth and not fabrications. They are to be trusted and revered.

Miraculous birth

It is not possible to prove or disprove historically or scientifically the miraculous virgin birth of Jesus. The tradition of the faith includes the veneration of Mary as the chosen instrument of God's incarnation in the world in the person of Jesus. The belief that Jesus was fully human and fully divine is essential to the whole understanding and purpose of Jesus. If God is God, there is nothing that limits God's ability to be conceived by the Holy Spirit in the womb of Mary. It becomes a matter of faith when we declare Jesus was born of the Virgin Mary. This completes the understanding of Jesus' nature from birth to death to resurrected life. When we receive the Holy Spirit by faith in Christ Jesus, we appreciate the virgin birth and the veneration of Mother Mary.

Safe from the enemy
The enemy of Jesus is "like a roaring lion." This predator is stalking us, looking for our weakness, and ready to devour our souls. We are safe from its power as long as we stand firm in our faith protected by "the full armor of God." When we go astray on our egocentric trips, we are vulnerable to these deceptions that lead to destruction. Keeping within the mighty fortress of the Christian faith is our salvation. When we have the Holy Spirit, we begin to know that we know, and our faith becomes our foundation for the process of sanctification.

CHAPTER 20

HEAVEN AND HELL

Jesus came into the world to radically transform the people of the world so that we might love God with all our hearts, minds, souls, and strength, and love our neighbors as ourselves. By knowing Jesus and following him, we will go to heaven for eternity, perfected by his grace. Jesus came to save all people from the consequences of sin and death. It is his desire that all people would be saved through him. Humans were created to be children of God, and to go to heaven when they leave this world. Humans were also given the wonderful gift of the freedom to choose God or to reject God. The gift of heaven is freely given. It is the greatest desire of all people who know Jesus Christ to offer this gift of eternal life in heaven to every person in this world. On that day that a lover of the Lord Jesus Christ goes to heaven, they will meet the people who they introduced to Jesus. They are the good and faithful servants of the Lord.

The topic of heaven has been described in the chapter on the kingdom of God. Jesus refers to the kingdom of heaven directly one hundred and nine times in the Gospels. He also refers to the kingdom of God, which is much the same thing, many more times. The subject of the reign of God (Kingdom) in this world and in the next was of primary importance to Jesus and his teachings.

Simply stated, heaven is where God reigns in every heart. Heaven is a world of light of God where there is no shadow. Although there is perfect compassion in heaven, there is no sorrow or suffering because of the great joy that exists in our communion with God. Everyone knows God's plan for the world in heaven and trusts it. Everything that is good, that is holy, that is beautiful, and that is godly is in heaven. Heaven is the most interesting and exciting place in the universe. In one billion years, one would not even begin to explore one segment of heaven. The ultimate glory of heaven is the centerpiece, which is to be directly in the presence of God. No one can imagine how wonderful heaven truly is. We either desire to go to heaven and strive with all our being to attaining heaven or we do not. The alternative to heaven is more terrible humans can imagine. Hell is separation from God. Jesus makes it absolutely plain to us that our choice is either heaven or hell. We are either moving towards God or away from God. Indifference is rejection of God.

In our hearts, we know whether we are heaven bound or we are not. When we ask Jesus Christ into our hearts, we are convicted of our sins, we repent, and we receive his redemption which is the forgiveness of our sins, and he will take us to heaven and perfect us. In John 17:1-3 (NRSV), "After Jesus had spoken these words, he looked up to heaven and said, 'Father, the hour has come; glorify your Son so that the Son may glorify you, since you have given him authority over all people, to give eternal life to all whom you have given him. And this is eternal life, that they may know you, the only true God, and Jesus Christ whom you have sent.'" No one can save us but Jesus, and we cannot save ourselves. If we had a million lifetimes, we could never save ourselves.

God created people so that they would go to heaven. It is God's desire that all people would choose heaven as opposed to hell. God has given every human being the tremendous gift of freedom to make that choice. God has created the standard that determines whether a person will go to heaven or to hell. For those who have had the opportunity to know the perfect revelation of God in Jesus Christ, we know exactly what the standard is. The standard is to love Jesus and to be obedient to his commandments. If we know Jesus, we will put all of our love, faith, trust, belief, and hope in him. Through the power of the Spirit of Christ, our lives are fruitful by loving God and loving our neighbor. We were not created to be isolated entities. God created us to live in relationship with one another so that we could help one another become the children of God. What we do with our lives determines whether we will go to heaven or hell when we die. In Matthew 7:18-20 (NRSV), Jesus states, "A good tree cannot bear bad fruit, nor can a bad tree bear good fruit. Every tree that does not bear good fruit is cut down and thrown into the fire. Thus you will know them by their fruits." Only good and fruitful people will go to heaven. Every human being is born with a capacity to be good and fruitful, and every human being is given the freedom to choose what kind of life they will lead. Our lives are judged by God's standard, and to know Jesus Christ is to know God's standards.

Jesus taught us the will of God in the way that he lived his life, in his teachings in the Bible, and through the Holy Spirit that he sends to us. Through Jesus, we know the perfect will of God, and we also know opposition to God. Sin is our intentional opposition and separation from God. Sin is a tremendous problem because it is a part of human nature and we need to recognize the power of sin in our lives and eliminate it. Jesus used the strongest possible imagery to convince us of the necessity of recognizing sin and overcoming it. Jesus says in Mark 9:43 (NRSV), "If your hand causes you to stumble, cut it off; it is better for you to enter life maimed than to have two hands and to go to hell, to the unquenchable fire." And in Mark 9:45 (NRSV), "And if your foot causes you to stumble, cut it off; it is better for you to enter life lame than to have two feet and to be thrown into hell." Also in Mark 9:47 (NRSV), "And if your eye causes you to stumble, tear it out; it is better for you to enter the kingdom of God with one eye than to have two eyes and to be thrown into hell." One cannot enter heaven if they have allowed sin to control their life. The privilege and blessing of going to heaven is a highly selective process and only those who have fought to rid their lives of sin will go to heaven. We are eager to find sin in other people, but slow to recognize the sin in ourselves. Jesus tells us unequivocally to rid the sin in our lives, and not be hasty in judging others.

The standard of Jesus Christ is very high and can only be obtained through the help of the Holy Spirit and forgiveness we receive. We have been taught by Jesus how to live and how to love one another. For example, he even teaches us that we should not even use abusive language towards anyone. In Matthew 5:22 (NRSV), "But I say to you that if you are angry with a brother or sister, you will be liable to judgment; and if you insult a brother or sister, you will be liable to the council; and if you say, 'You fool,' you will be liable to the hell of fire." The meaning of the word that is translated as "fool" was the word that meant a person was ungodly and incapable of knowing God. Jesus saw this kind of language as inexcusably hurtful towards another human being. We are judged by our thoughts, words, and deeds. Jesus teaches us that we are to strive for perfection, and even though we may not achieve perfection, it is to be our single goal in life to know and to do the will of God, which is perfection. Perfection is complete love of God and living accordingly.

It is critical to our attainment of heaven that we keep Jesus as our guide and standard. We are to have no other master or Lord other than Jesus. There are countless false teachers eager to lead us astray and they will promise anything, but they are all deceivers. The evil one is the ultimate master of deception and his followers have no truth in them. Their only ambition is to take others with them to where they're going, which is not to heaven. Jesus warns us in Matthew 10:28 (NRSV), "Do not fear those who kill the body but cannot kill the soul; rather fear him who can destroy both soul and body in hell." We must measure all things by Jesus Christ, and if it is not compatible with Jesus, the Jesus we know as revealed to us in the Gospels and by the Holy Spirit, then it is wrong. We must always test the spirits in the name of Jesus.

There is an abundance of false teachers in this world. And for everyone with the slightest inclination to be led astray, there are a multitude of temptations to lead them away from the path to heaven. Perhaps the most despicable are the false teachers who teach in the name of Christ. They use the name of Jesus but do not teach what he taught. They use religion for their own gain whether it is material wealth or the egotistical control of other people's lives. These counterfeit Christians proliferate today and some of them are extremely successful in fleecing their followers. Be warned by Matthew 23:15 (NRSV), "Woe to you, scribes and Pharisees, hypocrites! For you cross sea and land to make a single convert, and you make the new convert twice as much a child of hell as yourselves." Jesus warns anyone who is a teacher or a religious leader that they are accountable for what they teach and how they influence people. Jesus used the harshest language to condemn such people and warn us away from them, as in Matthew 23:33 (NRSV), "You snakes, you brood of vipers! How can you escape being sentenced to hell?" Each of us is responsible for our own lives because we have been equipped with the ability to reason for ourselves, and we all have access to the Spirit of Christ to discern the truth for ourselves. We have the Gospels to do a reality check on whether someone or something is consistent with the life of Jesus Christ and his teachings. If we are deceived, it is because we wanted to be deceived. Those who go to hell have chosen that path.

Separation from God

What is hell like? In the Christian tradition, there are many speculative theories about hell, but there is very little basis for these in the scriptures. The primary image of hell that Jesus used was to refer to the garbage dump outside of Jerusalem. The Valley of Hinnon (often translated as hell) was the municipal dump for

Jerusalem, which is what Jesus referred to most often as the opposite of Heaven. The Valley of Hinnon was a despised place because of the pagan practice of the sacrifice of children that was performed there before this area had been conquered by the Hebrew people. The inhabitants of Jerusalem had the waste products of human society collected and thrown into this place. The odor of the dump was horrible. There would have been smoldering fires and clouds of choking smoke that were never extinguished consuming some of the waste products. The organic garbage would have been covered in maggots. This dump bore no resemblance to a sanitary landfill. It was the most repulsive place imaginable. Jesus used the specific name for this dump "Gehenna" (Valley of Hinnon) as an image of hell, described in Mark 9:48 (NRSV), "where their worm never dies, and the fire is never quenched." A literal understanding of what Jesus was saying about hell is that it is being thrown into the filth of the rubbish pile. Whether hell is a place of worms and fire is not the point. Hell is a place of indescribable torment because it is complete separation from God and everything that God represents. In hell, a person suffers the consequences of their actions, where there is no hope. See and understand Matthew 25:41 (NRSV), "Then he will say to those at his left hand, 'You that are accursed, depart from me into the eternal fire prepared for the devil and his angels.'" Hell is a place for those who have rejected God. When we reject God, we choose hell as our destination. It is almost unthinkable that a person would choose to go to hell rather than go to heaven, but that is exactly what a person chooses when they reject God and the one whom God sent to save us. Jesus proclaims in John 15:6 (NRSV), "Whoever does not abide in me is thrown away like a branch and withers; such branches are gathered, thrown into the fire, and burned."

Another image that Jesus uses for hell is the image of darkness. In the Gospels, the contrast of light and darkness are frequently used to represent the difference between the godly and the ungodly.

The ungodly reject the light of God and crave the darkness; for example, John 1:4-5 (NRSV), "In him was life, and the life was the light of all people. The light shines in the darkness, and the darkness did not overcome it." Hell is the ultimate place of darkness because the light of God is not seen there. Explicitly stated Matthew 8:12 (NRSV), "While the heirs of the kingdom will be thrown into the outer darkness, where there will be weeping and gnashing of teeth." In this image of hell, there is terrible emotional torment in the pitch black night of the abyss. When a person dies having hated the light of God, they will have the darkness that they loved in this world, and the despair they suffer for the choices that they made.

The clearest description of heaven and hell that Jesus gave us is in the telling of the story of the beggar Lazarus and the rich man in Luke 16:22-31 (NRSV). "The poor man died and was carried away by the angels to be with Abraham. The rich man also died and was buried. In Hades, where he was being tormented, he looked up and saw Abraham far away with Lazarus by his side. He called out, 'Father Abraham, have mercy on me, and send Lazarus to dip the tip of his finger in water and cool my tongue; for I am in agony in these flames.' But Abraham said, 'Child, remember that during your lifetime you received your good things, and Lazarus in like manner evil things; but now he is comforted here, and you are in agony. Besides all this, between you and us a great chasm has been fixed, so that those who might want to pass from here to you cannot do so, and no one can cross from there to us.' He said, 'Then, father, I beg you to send him to my father's house— for I have five brothers—that he may warn them, so that they will not also come into this place of torment.' Abraham replied, 'They have Moses and the prophets; they should listen to them.' He said, 'No, father Abraham; but if someone goes to them from the dead, they will repent.' He said to him, 'If they do not listen to Moses and the prophets, neither will they be convinced even if someone rises from the dead.'"

From the words of Jesus, we learn important things. When the beggar died, he was carried to heaven by the angels. When we die, if we have accepted Jesus Christ as our Lord and Savior and followed his commandments, we will be carried by the angels to heaven. In heaven, Lazarus was in the company of the Saints of all time, and so shall we be also. The rich man went to hell where he was in torment because of his lack of charity, which is the act of love and compassion for the beggar outside of his door. In his agony, he called out for relief from his torment but was told that he was receiving his reward for his indifference (which is really contempt) for beggar outside his door. There is no interaction between heaven and hell. The rich man pleaded that Lazarus be sent to warn his five brothers so that they would not end up in hell. But he was told that they had Moses and the Prophets, they will not be convinced even if someone rises from the dead. So we have been warned by Jesus, who did rise from the dead, and still some of us are not convinced. Each of us is responsible for the choice that we make, and that choice has eternal consequences. May each one of us choose Jesus Christ as our Lord and Savior, and faithfully follow him to heaven.

Made in the USA
Coppell, TX
31 July 2024

35419415R00121